TRADITIONAL STORYTELLING

in the primary classroom

THE SCHOLASTIC

D0453112

© 1997 Teresa Grainger

Published by Scholastic Ltd
Villiers House
Clarendon Avenue
Leamington Spa
Warwickshire CV32 5PR

Author Teresa Grainger
Editor Clare Gallaher
Assistant Editor Kate Pearce
Series Designer Lynne Joesbury
Designer Louise Belcher

Designed using Aldus Pagemaker
Printed in Great Britain

The right of Teresa Grainger to be identified as the Author of this Work has been asserted by her in accordance with the Copyright, Designs and Patents Act 1988

British Library Cataloguing-in-Publication Data
A catalogue record for this book is available from the British Library.

ISBN 0-590-53686-9

ACKNOWLEDGEMENTS

There are many people to thank for encouraging and inspiring me, and enabling me to put pen to paper. The children and teachers I have worked with in Kent, Bexley, East Sussex and Croydon schools deserve first mention. In particular, Barbara Scott and her class at Beaver Green Juniors, Ashford; Jennie Bowen and her class at Hoath CP, Canterbury; Elaine Brasier and her class at St Stephens RCP, Bexley Heath; and Maisie Hookins and her class at Swanscombe Infants, Gravesend.

The London Narrative Group led by Harold Rosen at the Institute of Education has also been a source of support and solidarity and extended my understanding of the nature of oral narrative. For years Betty and Harold Rosen, Mike Hill, Jean Dunning, Doreen White, Mark Cremin and many others met to challenge one another's insights, share stories and undertake action research together. I learned a lot from these gatherings. Many thanks, too, to Sue Dunn, principal at Cedar Oak Park, Portland, Oregon and Janice Leonetti at Wilhamette Primary, Portland and the many other teachers, who have welcomed me into their schools, allowed me to work alongside their children and trusted the power of traditional storytelling. I would also like to thank Mark Cremin for his patience and faith in my work, to Canterbury Christ Church College for financial assistance, and to Gina Nuttall whose friendly encouragement has sustained me during the writing process.

The publishers would like to thank Richard Walker, publisher of the storytelling magazine *Facts and Fiction* in which 'Widsith's Pledge' appeared. After extensive efforts, the author of this version has not been able to be traced.

PRIMARY
PROFESSIONAL BOOKSHELF

CONTENTS

PRIMARY
PROFESSIONAL BOOKSHELF

PRIMARY
PROFESSIONAL BOOKSHELF

HOW THE TIDES CAME TO EBB AND FLOW
A traditional tale

Once in a place far from here, in a time when the earth was new, an ancient old woman had no hut to live in. She lived in the great outdoors among the animals and birds, on the wide open plains beside the sea. When the sun shone she was scorched, when the snow fell she was frozen, when the rain poured she was soaked and when the winds whistled across the plains she was bitterly cold. She suffered much because she had no home to protect her from the elements, and no friends or family save the wild creatures of the earth. Indeed, every day for as long as she could remember she had knelt and prayed to the great Sky Spirit To Whom all Things Belonged.

> *Sky Spirit, Sky Spirit*
> *Please hear my prayer.*
> *I'm alone and I'm homeless*
> *And need you to care.*

But the Sky Spirit, from his home in the heavens, always replied, 'No home today: try again tomorrow,' and the ancient old woman was left without a home.

One day, however, the woman had a bright idea (for all women are capable of such if left to their own devices) and on this day she knelt and prayed to the great spirit in the sky:

> *Sky Spirit, Sky Spirit*
> *Please hear my call.*
> *I need a large rock*
> *To give shelter to all.*

The Sky Spirit, surprised by her unusual request, replied, 'Take one, take one.' Let me tell you how happy the ancient old woman was then. A knowing smile spread across her face; her tired eyes twinkled with determination; her worn body knew it would soon find rest. She knew exactly which rock she was going to take, and so she rowed out into the ocean in her old stewpot. She rowed and she rowed, she rowed and she rowed, and soon who should she see but the Great Sea Bird who cawed:

> *Old Woman, Old Woman*
> *Please listen to me!*
> *You are rowing too close*
> *To the hole in the sea.*

'Aha!' answered the old woman. 'Then I think I am rowing in the right direction.

She rowed and she rowed, she rowed and she rowed, and soon who should she see but the Little Rainbow Fish who gurgled:

> *Old Woman, Old Woman*
> *Please listen to me!*
> *You are terribly close*
> *To the hole in the sea.*

'Aha!' answered the old woman. 'Then I *know* I am rowing in the right direction.'

When she reached a place where the water lay at ease with itself, her boat was becalmed. She peered down into the silent stillness and saw a rock more beautiful than any she had ever seen before. 'That is the rock, the rock I want,' she whispered, and she reached down towards it. But at that very moment the Sky Spirit To Whom All Things Belonged called to her from his home in the heavens:

> *Old Woman, Old Woman*
> *Now listen to me!*
> *DON'T take that rock*
> *From the hole in the sea.*

'But that's the rock, the rock I want,' the ancient old woman replied, and she reached down deep into the still waters. Then the Sky Spirit called again:

> *Old Woman, Old Woman*
> *Are you listening to me?*
> *Surely you're not taking*
> *The rock from the sea?*

'But that's the rock, the rock I want,' the ancient old woman replied, and she reached down deeper into the still waters. Then the Sky Spirit called for a third time:

> *Old Woman, Old Woman*
> *You're not listening to me;*
> *I'm telling you DON'T*
> *Take the rock from the sea!*

'But you said I could take one!' the clever old woman replied. She pulled and she heaved, she heaved and she pulled until *Sssloop*...! Out came the rock from the ocean floor. Then the Sky Spirit was sorry; the waters poured down and down through the hole in the sea.

The sea glugged and gurgled, the sea sucked and swirled and began to twist around and around, faster and faster as all the waters of the oceans rushed towards the hole. The stewpot was tossed in circles on the surface of the water, but the determined old woman held on tight to the rock.

'Put it back!' cried the Great Sea Bird and all the creatures of the air who were terribly afraid.

'Put it back!' cried the Little Rainbow Fish and all the creatures of the water, also terribly afraid.

'*Put it back!*' roared the furious Sky Spirit gathering the thunderclouds, but the old woman refused to put it back. 'It's mine now,' she called back to them.

So the Sky Spirit sent Little Dog down to earth: 'Go with haste, Little Dog, and put your nose in the hole in the sea.' Little Dog did as he was told, but his nose was too small and the water so cold. The oceans continued to pour through the hole, *slurrsh, slurrsh, slurrsh*, and Little Dog swam to the surface. The old woman took him in her stewpot and said, 'From now on you will be my little dog, and I will love you for always.'

So the Sky Spirit sent Young Maiden down to earth: 'Go with haste, Young Maiden, and kneel in the hole in the sea.' Young Maiden did as she was told, but her knees were too thin and the water so cold. The oceans continued to pour through the hole, *slurrsh, slurrsh, slurrsh*, and Young Maiden swam to the surface. The old woman took her in her stewpot and said, 'From now on you will be my daughter, and I will love you for always.'

In desperation the Sky Spirit sent Young Man down to earth: 'Go with haste Young Man and sit in the hole in the sea.' Young man did as he was told, but still the hole was too big and the water so cold. The oceans poured relentlessly through the hole, *slurrsh, slurrsh, slurrsh*, and Young Man swam to the surface. The old woman took him in her stewpot and said, 'From now on you will be my daughter's husband, and I will love you for always.'

Just then the waters began to swirl faster and faster, and the stewpot was tossed in ever decreasing circles towards the hole in the sea.

'Put back the rock!' cried all the creatures of the air.

'Put back the rock!' cried all the creatures of the sea.

'*Please* put back the rock,' cried the Sky Spirit, 'and I will let you borrow it twice a day forevermore.' The ancient old woman looked at Little Dog who would love and protect her, at Young Maiden who would talk to her when the chores were done and at Young Man, who would build her a hut, and she smiled and smiled. Then she reached over the side of the stewpot and replaced the rock in the hole in the sea, *phut!*

The waters stilled, the sea filled up and up, and the contented old woman rowed home with her new family. But from that day to this, the ancient old woman has borrowed that rock twice a day to pretty up her garden. As she removes the rock, the water goes down and down into the hole in the sea. That is low tide. When she replaces the rock, the sea fills up and up. That is high tide. To this day that is why the tides ebb and flow.

But some parts of Little Dog, Young Maiden and Young Man never did warm up. For to this day all dogs have cold noses, all maidens cold knees and all young men stand with their backs to the fire.

INTRODUCTION

It is the twilight hour. Two children prepare for bed. Lucy bangs the wooden bars of her cot, heralding her tale telling. Her brother Patrick looks up expectantly from his mug of milk as she announces, 'I do story a mouth. Lucy do it,' and proceeds:

> 'One morning... one morning long time ago... baby hippopotamus in river... he swim, splash, splash.'
>
> 'What happened next?' her brother enquires. 'Who came along?'
>
> Along come a crocodile, *snip! snap! snip! snap! snip! snap!* and eat up baby hippopotamus, *yum! yum!*
>
> 'Oh No! Poor baby hippopotamus. Why couldn't anyone have saved him? What happened?' Patrick demands to know.
>
> 'Along come a big giant elephant and picked up crocodile and spin and spin and baby hippopotamus pop out of mouth, and elephant throw crocodile high up in the sky and bad Mr Crocodile *never seen again*.'

The time, place and age of the storyteller and her audience may vary, but the power and existence of this oral tradition continues as a universal language habit. The nightly rituals of these two youngsters has always involved reading bedtime stories, with only the occasional retelling of tales. Now their parents find that this three-year-old and her older brother, who is four, demand *their* space in storytime to tell and retell tales. Their oral stories are a fascinating mixture of the real and the fictional, combining recent personal experience, significant memories, and the literature they have encountered. Oral stories speak directly to our senses, evoke feelings, demand imaginative engagement and foster the development of thinking, learning, language and literacy. Yet in primary schools the oral story tends to be somewhat neglected.

Young children like these pre-schoolers live in a world packed with stories: narratives of everyday events, anecdotes of family folklore, tales from the media and various other kinds of traditional stories experienced in school and out. Children learn to make sense of the world through constructing their own stories and through hearing tales from their own and others' literary heritage and culture. Folk tales, myths and legends passed down by word of mouth have been told and retold, formed and reformed over the centuries by countless tellers of all ages. Their themes and shapes echo across continents and cultures, and exist today, some still as spoken tales, many others as written and illustrated texts. However, as Tony Fairman, a storyteller, observes of traditional tales:

> ...a tale in a book is like a drum in a museum; it's silent, it's dead, it's just there doing nothing. And that's sad because tales are for telling; they're for laughter, they're for singing, for sharing.
>
> Fairman (1991)

Finding ways to share oral stories and bring them to life in the classroom is the central focus in this book, enabling children to tell and retell tales, and sing and dance them into existence. In doing so they can celebrate and savour the language of story, enhance their sense of self-identity and confidence, expand their story repertoire and develop their creative competence. Stories breed stories and sow in children the seeds of curiosity and challenge while simultaneously nurturing the growth of community, so traditional stories represent an explicit resource in the primary classroom and one which can be much more fully developed and explored.

This book seeks to encourage and inspire teachers to reinstate traditional oral storytelling as a powerful form of education and provide children with the chance to develop their natural narrative capacity and become the official storytellers in the classroom. The ancient tradition of storytelling and the nature of traditional tales is explored alongside the potential of this art form as a facilitator of language learning. Eight tales are offered for retelling drawn from different parts of the world, as well as a host of recommended anthologies, picture books and audio cassettes which can support classroom practice. A range of integrated language activities are shared for developing story writing and story reading as well as oral storytelling, and examples of children's work are provided to illuminate the nature of each practical activity. Drama is also examined as a tool for investigating folklore and developing the imagination in action. Frameworks for planning units of work on traditional storytelling into the primary curriculum are suggested in line with requirements and guidelines for English in the national curricula, and strategies to support teachers as well as children in the development of their confidence and competence as tellers of tales are examined.

The oral tradition of storytelling underpins and complements the growth of language and literacy. Its spellbinding power can liberate children's imaginations, release their creativity and enable them to weave dreams together, as they journey along this road of never-ending stories.

LADDER TO THE SKY
A North American Indian tale

L ong ago in the old forgotten time, in the days of the Great Manitou there
lived only strong and healthy people. The men were dark and brave, fast
of foot and sound of limb. They knew all the secrets of the forest which they
shared with their four-footed friends. The women, too, were strong and
lithe, tall in stature and sound in mind. Their nimble fingers wove reeds and
grasses into fine mats for their tepees. They gathered milkweed down to
make snug beds for their young, and shaped muk-kuks out of birch bark to fill
with all the plenty of woodland and stream.

At this time death was unknown, for these were the Anishinabe, the
original people, who the Great Manitou looked after as his own. He had
given to his people a physical link, a sacred vine which wove between his sky
kingdom and the earth. It was known as the Ladder to the Sky.

When people grew tired and old, a spirit messenger would descend the
vine and take them up to the heavens where they would dwell for ever in the
skies above. The Anishinabe were forbidden to touch this magic vine. Many
were the warning tales that parents told their young ones about the vine, and
many were the rituals performed to nurture it. It was a living ladder whose
secure roots dug deep into the earth and whose topmost tendrils trailed
around the highest star. Spirit messengers in the form of Indians were often
sent down the vine by the Great Manitou to visit his people. They would
walk through the villages speaking to everyone they met, for all were treated
equally in the eyes of the Great Manitou.

But one day, in one of the villages, discontent began to grow like a dark and
threatening shadow. People felt that one young man, who lived on the edge of
the village with his grandmother, was being favoured. Often, he was seen
walking with one of the spirit messengers; indeed, they were seen arm in arm,
and people began to talk. They muttered and they moaned, they wittered and
they wondered. What was it about this young man which made him so special?
Was it really a spirit messenger with him or merely a stranger? The people
were afraid of the spirits, but they were not afraid of the young man and, in
secret times and quiet places, they spoke unkind words, threw stones and
shunned his company.

The young man became a loner, without friends or companions save for his
grandmother. In time his lonely and melancholic thoughts were heard by the
Great Manitou, who sent a spirit messenger to bring him to live in the sky
kingdom for ever. The young man placed his hand in the shining hand of the
messenger and, despite his grandmother's protestations, he took his leave of
her. In a blinding flash of light he was gone.

'Be-ga-wain! Be-ga-wain! Come back! Come back!' the old woman
shrieked. But there was no answer.

That night, as darkness fell upon the village, the grandmother crept
stealthily and silently towards the forbidden vine. 'What is left for me in the

earth kingdom?' she asked herself. She had seen the half-jealous looks on the faces of the villagers. She had felt their hostility. Her grandson was her flesh and blood, her beloved one. She would go to him. As she reached for the fronds of the vine, it seemed to try to force her away, to repel her. But old women have a special force of their own, and with determination she grasped its leaves and wrapped her arms around its stem.

She climbed long and hard all through that fateful night, holding her grandson's face in her mind's eye and gripping each leaf and branch firmly as she ascended. When the sun rose, the Anishinabe saw the grandmother on the vine and, presuming the young man had climbed on ahead of her, the villagers cursed them and set fire to their lodge. At last the old woman reached the top of the vine where its final tendril was tied to a star. Her tired fingers reached out to pull her aching body past the star anchor and on to the floor of the sky kingdom. But the vine was not made for earth people to use and with a *snap!*, a splinter and a *crash!* their connection with the spirits was severed. The vine and the grandmother plummeted down towards the earth.

From all four corners of the Ojibway nation, from north, south, east and west, people gathered, forming a circle around the body of the old woman, around the cold ruins of the magic vine. What would happen to them now that their living Ladder to the Sky was no more? In solemn silence they wondered and waited, waited and wondered, until pain and discomfort began to strike first one and then another. Heads began to throb; arms began to ache; some could no longer walk; some could no longer speak. Now the people understood – disease and death were to be their punishment...

Many years later, the spirit messengers returned to the earth, bringing word from the Great Manitou that indeed disease and death would dwell for ever among his people. 'But,' said the spirits, 'the Great Manitou has sent us to show you how to reduce your pain and suffering.'

The spirits stretched out their fingers and, as they did so, flowers and plants from forest and plain, from river bank and woodland, came to settle in their palms. As these dried, the spirits blew on them and scattered these colourful fragments of nature all over the Ojibway lands.

'Each flower that buds can serve a wise and healing purpose,' they told the people. 'Each young leaf, strong stem and fragrant petal has the power to relieve your pain, to heal your wounds, to save your sons and daughters. Death will come to all until the end of time, but illness may now be treated. We will train some of your people to be the Midi-wi-win, the medicine men who will learn nature's sacred secrets. In their temple they will teach new generations these truths. From this time forward these secrets will be known to you and your people. From this time forward the Midi-wi-win will be able to help you. For you were never forgotten by the Great Manitou and through this act he has forgiven you.'

This happened many years ago, but the Ojibway people have never forgotten what they were taught, and even to this day they use the living power of nature to heal the sick and soothe their pain.

CHAPTER 1

STORYTELLING: AN ORAL TRADITION

Storytelling is an ancient art form, an integral part of human existence, and the most enduring form of education. It is an accessible and creative form of communicating and reflecting upon experience, both real and imagined, yet it is much more than this.

> Storytelling is the direct and shared communication of something true about being alive. It is not only the story, but a combination of a living storyteller, situation, sound and rhythm of voice, silence, gesture, facial expressions, and response of listeners that makes it potent.
>
> Laura Simms (1982)

This power and potency can be harnessed in the classroom through offering children the opportunity to tell and retell tales, and take an active part in this oral tradition. Hazel, a seven-year-old with special educational needs, delighted in the opportunity her class storytelling focus offered her. In her retelling, Hazel shared the tale of *The Wolf and the Seven Little Kids*. She sat perched on the edge of an old armchair in the book corner, her eyes alert, her pleasure and engagement obvious for all to see. Her friends sat at her feet listening, looking and imagining as Hazel let her tale unfold.

> Inside a little wood there was a little house, and inside that little house there lived a mother goat and her seven little kids. She never left them on their own for if she did the Big Bad Wolf would eat them *all* up! One day they had run out of sugar and they needed some more. The mother goat said to her little children, 'Listen carefully, we have run out of

sugar and we need some more. If the Big Bad Wolf comes you will know by his deep, raw voice and his black paw. Bolt the door as soon as I've gone.'

So the kids did what their mother said. No question!

But somehow or other, the wolf was hiding in the trees. When mother goat had gone and was out of sight, the wolf went up to the door and knocked. 'Open up, my dear, dear children, Mother's forgotten her purse. Let me in.'

The kids knew it was not their mother for the wolf had a big, raw voice and they replied, 'Go away, go away! We know you're the Big, Bad Wolf by your *deep, raw voice.*'

'So it's my voice – my voice has given me away. Some of that cough mixture from the chemist will do the trick,' the wolf thought.

The wolf came back again after drinking one, two, three bottles and knocked on the door again. And he said sweetly, 'Mother is back with some lovely pressies. Open up, my dear, dear children, let me in.'

Just at that moment the wolf put his big, black paw on the step. And the kids knew it was the wolf still and they replied, 'Go away, go away! We know you're the Big, Bad Wolf by your black paw.'

'So it's my paw – my paw has given me away this time. I'll put some flour all over my feet and then my feet will be white. So that should do the trick,' the wolf thought.

The wolf came back and knocked on the door for the third time and said sweetly, 'Open up, my dear, dear children, Mother's back from the shops.'

And the children replied, 'Let us see your paw.'

He put it on the step. It was white and therefore it must be their mother this time. So they unlocked the door, and... *in rushed the wolf!*

Three children hid in the bed, two in the linen basket, one hid under the table and one went up the clock. But it was no use! The wolf found them all – all except for one, the youngest of them all, the one who had hidden up the clock. When he heard that the wolf had gone and knew he was out of sight, he went to the step and waited for his mum. And when his mum returned, he ran up to her and told her all about the trick the wolf had played.

The mother goat and her little son went for a walk in the wood, and then the little goat shouted, 'Look, look over there, under the apple tree, it's the Big, Bad Wolf and the fat tummy which has all my brothers and sisters in!' And sure enough it was the wolf. They ran up to him. He was snoring. *Sn... Sn... Sn... sssh.*

'Quickly! Fetch my scissors, my cotton and needle!' the mother goat said.

The little goat ran to the house and ran back with the scissors, cotton and needle. He gave the scissors, cotton and needle to his mum. She slit open his tummy and out popped the little kids. *Hurrah! Pop! Pop! Pop! Pop! Pop! Pop!* She then said, 'Quickly! Fetch me some stones from the river.' They were heavy, but they soon managed to put them in his tummy, and the mother goat sewed them up and they went skipping back home together, *Tra-la Tra-la Tra-la.* And with the sugar the mother had bought she made some toffee apples, *Yum, Yum.* They were yummy indeed.

Meanwhile, back at the wolf. He became thirsty and needed some water. So he went up to the river and drank, and then suddenly he lost his balance and went SPLASH! BANG! He was DEAD! DROWNED!

Mother goat is often seen in the town nowadays, for the Big, Bad Wolf is finally dead and gone for ever.

Hazel's pleasure and power in telling her tale is only partially portrayed in the transcript; the tape itself carries her wealth of intonation patterns, voices for the characters, volume variations and dramatic pauses which cleverly convey her tale. The repetitive language of oral stories scents her retelling ('*my dear, dear children*' and '*so it's my voice — my voice has given me away*' and *'so it's my paw – my paw has given me away'*) and she builds up moments of dramatic tension most effectively, holding the audience with her sense of urgency, anticipation and awareness of climax. Her only visible props were seven strips of paper on which she had drawn the sequential elements of the narrative. In the event she hardly referred to them, embellishing and enlivening this folk tale herself with her own spoken language and gesture. Like her classmates, Hazel was able to take a fuller and more confident part in this activity than in many others across the curriculum, for as an oral storyteller already, she could build upon her ability, communicate easily in this form and develop personal confidence and pleasure in her success. Hazel, like many before her across the centuries, was taking part in the oral tradition of storytelling, and was able to retell the tale afresh and shape it at the very moment of utterance in interaction with her audience. She was and is a storyteller.

It is to the past, to the ancient oral tradition of storytelling that this chapter now turns to examine the historical development of traditional storytelling and key features of traditional tales.

TRADITIONAL STORYTELLING: PAST AND PRESENT

Before the written word, knowledge about the world, explanations of natural phenomena, the laws and history of different peoples, their gods, origins, fears and hopes were shared by word of mouth as oral stories. In the beginning, everyone was a storyteller, using the spoken word and narrative to communicate, educate and entertain. Gradually, however, over time, particular individuals began to elevate and refine their skills, singing or chanting their stories and establishing themselves as significant and respected storytellers within their communities. As time passed, the stories they told became a mêlée of anonymous personal tales, myths and legends, tales of heroism and of the past expressed in verse, in prose and song. The stories travelled too, from one land to another, from one century to the next, transforming and reforming as they did so, shaped by countless tellers and listeners across the continents and through the centuries. All over the world, storytellers existed as historians, entertainers, upholders of moral values, repositories of religious knowledge and bringers of news.

DIFFERENT TRADITIONS OF STORYTELLING

The Bardic tradition of storytelling involved poets and singers performing oral stories about noble heroes from the past. In Wales the apprentice bards had to learn multitudes of tales and train for twelve years to become masters of their craft. In India the early wandering bards, called *magadha*, were much revered, and in Ireland the *ollam* was looked on as the poet laureate of his day. In Russia the *skomorokhi* performed for wide audiences and held much status, as did the *skalds* and *sagas* of the Northern Lands who held a privileged position in the king's retinue. These 'professional' storytellers were polished performers, who often used musical instruments to enhance their tales. In Anglo-Saxon England storytellers were known as *gleemen*. The words of one such gleeman, known as Widsith, from the eleventh century, offer an evocative pledge passed down from that time.

I am Widsith:

Word shaper, hoarder of tales; one who sings, one who can see:

When I was young, my songs were called in the mead hall:

I gave peace to the bereft and the forsaken, merriment to the meek,

hope to ragged men who had no lord:

I, Widsith, the far-mover say this:

I have roamed through all the lands of our kin,

mingled with all the folk that men know, journeyed till my bones ache:

I have stood long in the Great Hall before my master the keeper of our kin;

yet I kneel before the bright stone:

I left the land where my children were princes, with the fair
peace-weaver;

whose arm by my back and breath on my neck gave me
strength:

From the world of wyrd I gathered much; charms for grace
to make good things grow,

spells to sting witches, fables to give strength to wind blown
striplings:

Will you hear me?

For those that will, your hearth will not be lonely:

I shall weave thick webs for the treacherous, wisdom for
the innocent, riddles for the curious:

I will break stone hearts with grief, jest with great ones,
pluck roses for lovers:

And so I unlock my word hoard.

Be still and listen.

Later, the term *gleeman* was replaced by the Norman name *minstrel*. These travelling storytellers also narrated their tales in verse, chant and song, and often worked in groups, performing acrobatics and dramatics as well as stories. Such minstrels and master storytellers were found in many countries, where there was also a wealth of other traditions.

Religious storytelling represents a different tradition through which faith leaders and teachers explained their religion in stories. As the oral story engaged listeners very effectively and shared symbolic meanings, it was seen as a useful tool with which to promote religion. For example, the Hindu epics of The Mahabharata and The Ramayana were composed to introduce the sacred texts to the people, and the Hasidic Jews told oral tales to introduce their religion and its practices to children. The Christian oral stories of the Old and New Testament also represent examples of religious storytelling, although some scholars argue that parts of the Gospel texts were, in fact, composed by a writer.

Folk storytelling has an ancient tradition also, and includes storytelling that took place in homes, market places and in the streets, as well as other social gatherings, when mainly untrained tellers shared their stories with children and adults. Family storytelling still has a high priority in many parts of Africa and special names are given to describe such family gatherings. The Edo of Benin, Nigeria, for example, call such an event an *ibota*. Telling children stories is also a feature in native American contexts and among the Australian aborigines who, as Pellowski (1990) notes, would illustrate their tale telling with evocative drawings in the sand. There were and are a wealth of other examples of folk storytelling, since tales were told by commonfolk in nearly every country in the world.

THE INFLUENCE OF THE PRINTED WORD

In England, however, the coming of print in the fifteenth century heralded the demise of the tradition of oral storytelling, and scholars began to record the stories. So the written story also became a resource for handing tales down from generation to generation. Traditional tales, myths, legends, folk and fairy tales continued to be shared for some time but gradually, in England, the initial custom of oral storytelling declined, and in many places almost disappeared. The demise of the oral tradition coincided with the invention of artificial lighting. As Padriac Colum (1948) observed, the decline of storytelling has also been linked to the changing work patterns attached to the Industrial Revolution. In the mid-nineteenth century, traditional tales from the European tradition were collected for posterity by folklorists and anthropologists who rewrote and edited these oral stories for a specifically children's audience. Many of the tales were 'sanitised', reduced to a small fragment of their former selves, and the roles of certain characters were reshaped according to the expectations and moral codes of the day. Out of this work came the written collections of the Brothers Grimm, Joseph Jacobs and many others which in themselves became the basis of contemporary twentieth-century retellings.

So it is argued, with some truth, that

> All printed texts of folk tales are compromises between the written and the spoken word, between writers and storytellers.

Glassie (1986)

In many other countries, the seams of the oral tradition ran much deeper, and the tales and the practice of storytelling managed to survive more successfully alongside the printed word. Although books, and later television, appeared, the tradition has endured in many cultures, and stories still exist by being passed on orally. A symbiotic relationship developed between the oral tradition and written literature and this continues today. The variety in living storytelling styles and traditions across the world is immense. For example, the energy and physical involvement of many African calypso tale tellers demands both audience interaction and immediate response. In contrast, the reflective tale telling of a Celtic traveller sitting beside a community campfire offers a more intimate, less physical style, and the shadow puppets, masks, song and dance involved in much Asian and Far Eastern storytelling creates a still different and more literally visual sense of performance. This diversity represents a small selection of the styles and traditions practised and performed across the world, and encourages teachers to value the range of languages, patterns and cultural customs within this ancient art form.

A MORE CONTEMPORARY PERSPECTIVE

As the next millennium approaches, the art of oral storytelling is undergoing a remarkable revival in Britain. No doubt influenced by the more multicultural nature of its society, the songs, riddles, myths, legends, tales and history of all its people are becoming woven into the contemporary tapestry of storytelling in Britain. The older, unbroken oral traditions of the Irish and Scottish traveller folk, which never completely disappeared, are also contributing to this renaissance. The seeds of storytelling are germinating rapidly, with women tale tellers stepping forward to take a more public role than before and, as the storyteller Mary Medlicott (1989) observed, there has been the emergence of 'a completely new breed of storytellers who come from no one tradition but are born from the eclectic mix of modern urban life'.

Britain seems to be following in the footsteps of earlier revivals in Canada and the United States. Indeed, the whole of the Western world is showing a growing interest in storytelling, perhaps responding to a reawakened aesthetic and human need for telling and listening to stories. Whatever the reason for the rejuvenation, the power of storytelling is being discussed, developed and enjoyed in many different forums. In psychotherapy contexts and rehabilitation centres, in pubs and clubs, in libraries and art centres as well as in homes and schools, oral stories are today being told and retold, acted, sung, chanted, danced and devoured. To encapsulate this range and promote the diversity, variety and depth of storytelling, the Society for Storytelling was established in 1993. It has become a forum for the exchange of information and represents storytelling across a wide spectrum: as a high performance art form, as a form of therapy, as an educational tool and much more besides. The Society seeks to value, protect and enhance the 'oralness' of this art form and is also contributing to the revival of storytelling currently taking place in schools. National curricula and guidelines in England, Wales, Scotland and Northern Ireland all accord storytelling status within the development of speaking and listening, and the pleasure and educational potential of the oral story is being reacclaimed.

THE NATURE OF TRADITIONAL TALES

Traditional tales are tales which belong to the oral tradition of storytelling, tales which have been handed down by word of mouth through successive generations and across different cultures. Such stories, polished in different ways, are clearly as ancient and modern as the art of storytelling itself. A vast range of stories exist within the oral tradition including riddles and jokes, personal anecdotes and family stories, folk and fairy tales, and myths and legends. In Ireland this span of stories is called *a ladder to the moon*, which suggests that the first rung starts with human stories on earth and the last rung reaches the moon, with stories of its origin. Many such traditional tales have been published as printed literature, and have been reshaped and recorded in different forms.

TRADITIONAL TALES ARE TRAVELLERS

In essence, traditional tales refer to myths, legends, fables, folk and fairy tales. Such tales have deep roots embedded in the reality of mankind long ago, but have been altered by the traditions, cultures and histories they have inhabited. Many of these tales are carriers of culture, since they often bear witness to the knowledge, wisdom, social practices and beliefs of the people who gave birth to them. Storytelling is a way of preserving, sharing and celebrating the cultural heritage of all people, and can introduce children to other cultures and to the heroes of different mythologies which exist across the world. In fact, some folk tales have become cross-cultural narratives as they have journeyed and been retold by different tellers.

> By all accounts, *Cinderella* is the best-known fairy tale, and probably also the best-liked. It is quite an old story; when first written down in China during the ninth century AD, it already had a history. The unrivalled tiny foot size as a mark of extraordinary virtue, distinction, and beauty, and the slipper made of precious material are facets which point to an Eastern, if not necessarily Chinese, origin. The modern hearer does not connect sexual attractiveness and beauty in general with extreme smallness of the foot, as the ancient Chinese did, in accordance with their practice of binding women's feet.
>
> Bettelheim (1991)

Across the known universe, similar stories are found which assume a variety of forms, since in the voices of parents and grandparents, friends and relatives, travellers and others, they have been transformed. Written records of these tales have also transformed them. However, as Hugh Lupton (1995), a storyteller, observed at a time of telling of tales,

> Standing immediately behind us are all those who have told and retold this story before; we must remember them.

VARIETIES OF TRADITIONAL TALES

The fine differences between folk and fairy tales, myths and legends are the focus of considerable debate, but all reflect communal ways of making sense of experience. These tales have survived not only because they entertain, inspire, challenge and please people, but also because they offer alternative worlds which embody imaginative, emotional and spiritual truths about the universe.

Folk tales emerged from the need that communities have for sharing their wisdom and experience in a memorable manner, and are a central resource for storytelling in education, particularly in multicultural classrooms where, for example, Afro-Caribbean and Asian children have direct links with their influential oral traditions. Animals frequently feature in folk tales alongside, or instead of, humans, both of whom succeed through their quick-wittedness, or use of some kind of trick. Examples of tales about tricksters include *Ananse*, the spider man from Africa, *Coyote*, the clever wolf from North America and *Baba Yaga*, the iron-toothed witch from Russia.

Fairy tales are also folk narratives and open up the world of magic, of kings, queens, little people and the supernatural. These often retain the refrains and structures of folk tales. Examples include the many written tales originally recorded by historians and scholars, like *Rapunzel*, *Snow White* and *Hansel and Gretel* published by the Brothers Grimm. *The Wild Swans*, *The Tinder Box* and *The Snow Queen* by Hans Christian

Andersen built on this tradition. The anthropologist Andrew Lang also collected fairy tales and published these, alongside Joseph Jacob's *English Fairy Tales*. Later, more explicitly invented fairy tales emerged like Oscar Wilde's *The Happy Prince* and *The Selfish Giant*.

Legends and sagas usually refer to kings, great heroes and others who lived in the periods before written records. Examples include the many legends of King Arthur and the Holy Grail, the Greek legends of the Trojan War, and the legendary lives of Theseus and Jason as well as the Chippeweyan legend of the *Ladder to the Sky* (see pages 11–12). More recently, urban and local folk legends have also emerged. Examples include *The White Lady of Pluckley* and *The Beast of Bluebell Hill, Chatham*.

Myths tend to refer to stories which explain the origins of natural and supernatural phenomena, and human and superhuman characteristics. The ancient myths arose out of religious rites which offered people the chance to explain the spiritual side of life. These tales are challenging to tell, and often have a more complex narrative structure and more demanding language than folk tales. Examples include the Greek and Norse myths; the great Hindu myths (the Mahabharata and the Ramanyana); and the aboriginal myths, an example of which, entitled *How the Sun Came into the World* is included in this book (see pages 144–5).

Fables are often very short tales with overt morals, few characters and a strong element of the fabulous. The most common of these are by Aesop and La Fontaine, although there are established fables in other countries of the world. Examples include *The Hare and the Tortoise* and *The Fox and the Grapes*.

Epics are stories which were composed as poetry. Examples include *The Sundiata*, that is, the great epic of Mali, *The Odyssey* and the tale of *Beowulf*, the famous epic from the North.

Ballads are closely related to tales of heroes and epics, and are sung or chanted to recount heroic deeds. Examples include *The Ballad of Dan McGrew* and *The Ballad of Fin McCoul*.

Tall tales are those in which exaggeration has run riot and the story has become extravagant, nonsensical and yet entertaining. Examples of tall tales include Raspe's exploits of *Baron Munchausen* and the more modern American tales of *Paul Bunyan* and *Davy Crockett*.

THEMES IN TRADITIONAL TALES

Traditional tales deal with powerful archetypal issues and can give children insights into the patterns and motives of human behaviour. They explore such themes and universals as:

✧ good and evil;

✧ the nature of the supernatural;

✧ the origins of the earth and of man;

✧ rich and poor;

✧ young and old;

✧ beauty and ugliness;

✧ animals as helpers of people;

✧ the quest to test individual skill;

✧ the journey as a symbol for self-discovery.

Oral stories can give children easy access to complex issues which challenge the human race. The sense and meaning conveyed are not necessarily carried by the plot or the sequence of events, but are invested in the human qualities, the predicaments of the characters and the metaphoric nature of the language. Through exploring issues such as justice and injustice, and the moral codes of the characters, ethics and values can be examined and bridges between reality and fantasy built.

Bruno Bettelheim (1991) in his seminal text entitled *The Uses of Enchantment* argues that fairy tales make a significant contribution to children's psychological growth. His Freudian analysis of these tales suggests that they enable children to come to terms with the dilemmas of growing up, and are vital for their emotional development. He also argues clearly in favour of telling such tales to children and not reading them, noting that the interactional nature of storytelling provides flexibility and interpersonal insight between parent and child.

Listening to a fairy tale and taking in the images it presents may be compared to a scattering of seeds, only some of which will be implanted in the mind of the child. Some of these will be working in his conscious mind right away; others will stimulate processes in his unconscious. Still others will need to rest for a long time until the child's mind has reached a state suitable for their germination, and many will never take root at all. But those seeds which have fallen on the right soil will grow into beautiful flowers and sturdy trees – that is, give validity to important feelings, promote insights, nourish hopes, reduce anxieties – and in doing so enrich the child's life.

Bettelheim (1991)

Jungian psychoanalytical views also see the fairy tale as an expression of enrichment and personal development. In addition to this psychological perspective, traditional storytelling encourages a licence to wonder at the mystery and uniqueness of life. This is what Elizabeth Cook (1969) describes as 'religio', the intangible sense of knowing which lies beyond human personality, in the numinous and the mystical.

STEREOTYPING IN TRADITIONAL TALES

The nature of traditional tales is to invite interpretation, not to provide it, so they make excellent material for storytelling in the classroom. However, such tales are not without their problems, particularly in relation to stereotyping. The implicit messages about gender roles and personality traits ascribed to males and females have often been criticised in folk and fairy tales. It is true that the beautiful princesses waiting to be rescued by gallant princes, the cruel stepmothers and adventurous young men who tend to inhabit these tales generally reflect a dominant male ideology. Contemporary society affords women more complex roles than the societies in which the tales were recorded, and indeed men who do not wish to develop the powerful physical prowess perceived to be the male ideal are also compromised by such stereotyping. In addition, character traits are often polarised and individuals presented as either extremely good or very bad. In some traditional tales race and class stereotypes also exist.

However, teachers can use such tales to raise awareness of these issues and prompt discussion of the various different stereotypes. Children's knowledge of the world of folklore and fantasy may mean such dilemmas can be more easily raised, debated and understood than in other contexts. As storytellers themselves, children can use the tradition's propensity to embellish, make alterations and develop different orientations in their own retellings. They can also be introduced to collections which provide alternative role models. Teachers can help children to become responsive and critical readers through examining folk tales which are part of their corporate heritage. As the Asian storyteller Beulah Candappa notes, bridges of understanding between cultures can be built through the use of traditional tales.

> Through storytelling for children and adults, whilst rejoicing at the diversity I find all around, I am also singing praises to what binds us together. For, in spite of apparent differences – cultural, racial, religious – it is the same emotions which move people worldwide: joy, pain, sorrow, fear, hope, hate, love. The themes are universal. We share a common humanity. 'Above all nations is humanity.'
>
> Beulah Candappa (1989)

STRUCTURES IN TRADITIONAL TALES

Traditional tales often have distinctive story patterns and narrative structures which help both the teller and listener remember and enjoy the tale. Vladimir Propp (1968) studied a printed selection of Russian folk tales and concluded that there are only thirty-one different possible plots in such tales. This suggests that once children have become familiar with such plots, they can use them to predict the nature of other tales and the action within them. This structuralist perspective also proposes that it is not only the plots of traditional tales which remain relatively constant but also the kinds of characters that exist within them.

Certainly it is the case that many folk tales possess particular story patterns which increase their memorability and predictability. For example, in cumulative tales elements are added as the story progresses, and these prompt the audience to join in with the chronological chanting and encourage them to guess how often the pattern will be repeated. Examples include *The House that Jack Built*, *The Great Big Enormous Turnip* and *The Musicians of Bremen*. Sequential stories are also highly predictable, and involve a single event being repeated several times; the same words recur on each occasion as the story advances. Examples include *The Three Billy Goats Gruff*, *Gone is Gone* and *Molly Whuppy*. Number pattern stories are also common (although these may also be cumulative or sequential tales). Their number reliance aids the teller's recall and helps to organise the action. Examples include *The Fisherman and his Wife*, *Goldilocks and the Three Bears* and *Mrs Goat and her Seven Little Kids*. In European cultures the number 3 frequently occurs in traditional tales as do the numbers 7 and 13. In many cultures, 3 has some religious significance. Journeys also offer a common structure to folk tales, myths and legends: journeys to recover what is lost as in *The Ladder to the Sky*, journeys to other lands as in *The Weaving of a Dream*, and journeys to test and prove as in *The Final Victory*, all in this book (see pages 11, 161 and 95).

Traditional tales use a variety of combinations of these and many other story structures, but the repetitive, sequential and accumulating patterns of simple folk tales in particular make them suitable for young children to retell. These tales show strong similarities to playground rhythms and rhymes, extend children's ability to memorise lists, and involve young learners in linguistic and semantic experimentation which is both easily possible and immensely pleasurable.

THE LANGUAGE OF TRADITIONAL TALES

Another feature of the stories of the oral tradition is found in the memorable language used. The language of traditional tales abounds with symbol, metaphor, imagery, intertextuality and oblique meanings, and is a rich contributor worth savouring. Set openings and endings, rhythmic and repetitive refrains and repeated phrases often mark the pattern of events, and please the ear, evoking a physical response, a strong sense of structure and vivid images.

Alfred Lord (1960), in studying the epic poets of mid-twentieth century Yugoslavia, observed that poems of remarkable length were learned quickly by these often illiterate performers because they already knew the oral formulae and structural frameworks of such epics. Children rapidly and tacitly learn the structures and language patterns of traditional tales if they are given the chance to hear them, play with them and retell them. Such tales were originally moulded for the ear and those with a strong oral orientation still retain considerable repetition, rhythm and rhyme. This often prompts a more active engagement in the story since the repeated words and chants offer the audience the opportunity to join in, to journey alongside the storyteller and to taste the flavour and poetic resonance of the language.

The repetitive language propels some tales along and also provides breathing spaces in the narrative, during which the audience chant the refrain and simultaneously predict and reflect on the story. The use of idiomatic language conveyed with intonation, expression, and non-verbal sounds gives vitality and energy to tales. The often direct and lively language of oral stories, the people's vernacular, is frequently echoed in written versions, and is evident in many oral story tapes. This link between the spoken story and the written story has always been present and there is no absolute division between the oral and literate traditions. So the nature of the poetic, evocative and naturally metaphorical language of traditional tales aids memorisation and creative written retellings.

TRADITIONAL TALE TELLING: IN CONCLUSION

Folk and fairy tales, myths and legends are accessible in style and structure, rich in poetic intensity and are built around universal themes. They represent rich material in the primary classroom for teachers and children to build upon.

> Stories that lead to doing things are all the more attractive to children, who are active rather than passive creatures. Myths and fairy tales provide an unusually abundant choice of things to do. Largely because they are archetypal and anonymous (in quality, if not in provenance), they will stand reinterpretation in many forms without losing their character. They can be recreated by children not only in words but in drama, in mime, in dance and in painting. Action in them is not fussy, and lends itself to qualitative expression in the movements of the human body and in the shapes and colours of non-figurative painting.
>
> Cook (1969)

Traditional tales can open doors into many different art forms, the most significant of which is the oral tradition of storytelling, of sharing tales through the spoken word. In becoming traditional storytellers, children engage in the time-honoured process of retelling, revisiting and recreating the folklore of their common culture in interaction with their audience. The creative interplay which develops between the storyteller and the audience during traditional storytelling, and the immediacy and intimacy of the situation, fosters the creative tendencies of the teller and the listener and creates a shared imaginative experience. Storytelling is a social process and needs to be acknowledged as an active and interactive art form which creates a common bond between teller and told.

THE END OF BABA YAGA
A Russian tale

In a land far from here, there once lived three sisters – well, two sisters and one stepsister, to be exact. Vasseila, the youngest, was beautiful, and one thing her sisters could not abide was beauty. Every day she was forced to work her fingers to the bone for her sisters: washing, cooking, ironing, cleaning, tidying and tending to their every need. However, she accepted her place in the world with good grace and served her sisters with a smile. Yet Vasseila ached for a friend to talk to, a confidante or companion, someone she could trust.

One night, as she sat sewing by the fire, her sisters plotted to be rid of her. They planned to dampen down the fires, extinguish all the candles and send Vasseila out into the darkness to fetch light from Baba Yaga's house at the other side of the forest. Baba Yaga was well known in those parts. She held the only source of light for miles around, but she was also a witch woman with iron teeth and had the unpleasant habit of eating people! The sisters gloated together at the prospect of being rid of this smiling sibling, their stunningly lovely stepsister.

The desperate scheme went according to plan. They starved the fire and blew out most of the candles. Then, in an apparent fit of sneezing, the eldest sister spat out the last wick and Vasseila was sent in search of light.

'Why not try Baba Yaga's house?' her sisters suggested as she drew her thin cloak around her and disappeared into the blackness of the night. 'Hurry girl, hurry!'

Vasseila did hurry, for the icy wind whipped at her ankles and stung her bare skin. She stumbled through the edge of the wood until she heard the heavy fall of horses' hooves upon the earth. Cowering behind a tree, Vasseila watched as a great white knight on a pure white stallion galloped past her heralding the misty daylight which followed in his footsteps.

The morning mists cleared gradually and she was able to make her way through the forest with relative ease. Later, resting for a while on some moss, Vasseila was disturbed by the beating of hooves again. This time a scarlet knight riding a chestnut mare hastened past her and the sun set in his wake. As Vasseila clambered to her feet and set off down the path, a third horseman thundered by. As the dust kicked up by the black horse and his rider settled, darkness reigned. Vasseila was once again alone, but this time on the other side of the forest.

There before her stood a house perched upon a cockerel's foot which twisted this way and that. Vasseila knew this was Baba Yaga's house; she saw the bone fence, the gate whose catch was composed of a human hand (all flesh removed) and the seven skulls around the door. The sockets where their eyes had once been glowed with a knowing strength; it felt as though they were watching her. Determinedly, however, Vasseila pressed on. Avoiding the gate, she climbed through the fence and peeped in the windows. There she saw a young girl about her own age sitting alone by the fire sewing. Vasseila knocked and was welcomed inside by Baba Yaga's daughter. The two girls talked and talked, shared tales and memories, and much laughter. The time sped by and it wasn't long before Baba Yaga came rowing home across the sky in her pestle and mortar. Her daughter, afraid lest her mother should find her new friend, turned Vasseila into a sewing needle and stuck her in a pin cushion.

'Do I smell human flesh?' her mother demanded to know.

'Oh no, Mother, it was but a... passing stranger. He has gone now,' replied her daughter.

When Baba Yaga rowed away in the morning, Vasseila was returned to her human form and the two girls spent many happy hours together, baking and sewing, chatting and dancing until, hearing the witch woman's cackle, Vasseila was changed into a needle once again. On the third day the girls were so involved in what they were doing that they did not notice that the suspicious Baba Yaga had silently returned down the chimney. She leaped into the room with glee.

'My dinner,' she announced, grinning menacingly at Vasseila. She instructed her daughter to stoke up the fire and told Vasseila to sit upon a large wooden spatula. She intended to bake her in the oven! Vasseila obliged, but her legs hung over the edge.

'Sit the other way, girl!' commanded Baba Yaga, and Vasseila turned. But still her legs dangled over the edge and she could not be pushed into the oven.

'Let me show you,' screeched Baba Yaga impatiently, and sat upon the wooden spatula with her legs tucked up in front of her. Seizing their chance, the two girls shoved Baba Yaga into the oven and clanked shut the iron door.

They raced out of the house, stopping only to take some lace, a cake and a single skull. They knew that Baba Yaga could chew her way out of the oven and, as they ran along the forest paths, they heard her awful voice shrieking behind them as she gave chase. She was gaining on them when Vasseila dropped the lace woven in friendship. Where it fell a huge lake opened up and Baba Yaga was forced to swim across it.

Now swimming is slower than running, but once out of the water Baba Yaga caught up with them again. Desperately Vasseila dropped the cake baked in companionship. An enormous mountain arose behind them and Baba Yaga was forced to gnaw her way through, rocks and all.

As they reached the other side of the forest, the girls saw the stepsisters' home. They dropped the skull and its eyes glowed, throwing a ball of fire towards the house which ignited instantly. Where the skull hit the ground a huge void opened up and the screaming witch woman fell down, deep down into the dark chasm which quickly closed over and around her. She was trapped beneath the earth's crust, held tight for ever within the rock strata.

But it is said that if you visit a forest and see a single weed growing alone, outside the company of others, you may have stumbled on the spirit of Baba Yaga who continues to search for a way out. Be wary of where you tread!

CHAPTER 2

STORYTELLING: A LEARNING TRADITION

The history of traditional storytelling suggests that there may be an unconscious human need for story, for the insights stories offer and the doors into learning they push ajar. Storytelling can be a powerful way to engage children's imagination and help them learn in all areas of the curriculum, as the philosopher Keran Egan (1988) has argued in his influential text *Teaching as Storytelling*. In preliterate societies storytelling was a highly significant form of education. Today its potential remains largely undeveloped in the context of the classroom. Right across the curriculum, children are expected to hypothesise, predict, organise their ideas and give structure to their thinking and writing, and they rely upon their narrative competence to achieve this.

> ...the practice of narrating stories, either invented or retold, helps young children to come to know what it is to think through problems, argue cases, see both sides of questions, find supporting evidence, and make hypotheses, comparisons, definitions, and generalizations.
>
> Fox (1990)

Underpinning this claim is the relationship between narrative and cognition and the significant role that narrative plays in helping children to shape experience and make meaning for themselves. This chapter seeks to examine the narrative habit and to identify the multiple language and literacy competencies which children develop when they engage in telling stories: personal stories about everyday living and traditional stories about the human condition. Narrative is central to early learning and thinking, and teachers can build upon this.

STORYTELLING AT HOME AND AT SCHOOL

> My argument is that narrative, like lyric or dance, is not to be regarded as an aesthetic invention used by artists to control, manipulate or order experience, but as a primary act of mind transferred to art from life... What concern me here are the qualities which fictional narrative shares with that inner and outer storytelling that plays a major role in our sleeping and waking lives. For we dream in narrative, daydream in narrative, remember, anticipate, hope, despair, believe, doubt, plan, revise, criticise, construct, gossip, learn, hate, and love by narrative. In order really to live, we make up stories about ourselves and others, about the personal as well as the social past and future.
>
> Hardy (1977)

As Hardy observes, all humans engage in inner and outer storytelling and through this process build their experience of living, give order to chaos, structure their identity, and make sense of both lived and vicarious experience. Bruner (1987) too acknowledges that narrative is closer to cognition than has traditionally been recognised and proposes the existence of two modes of thought: a logical scientific mode, and a narrative mode of thinking and searching for understanding.

Scholars from a multitude of disciplines, from psychology, sociology, anthropology, theology and history, as well as those concerned with language and literature argue that narrative is central to the operation of the human mind. As H. Rosen (1984) argues, it is an *irrepressible genre,* a major means of thinking, communicating, and making meaning. Young children develop this narrative competence early, since, as they learn to speak they learn to tell stories, partly through hearing stories of all sorts in many different social contexts. Their desire to communicate and to socialise prompts them to join in, and the rules and skills they need to participate are learned in interaction.

Home is a place where stories are told. This is a
fundamental definition of home which is not in the
dictionaries. A family lives by its stories. Without them it is
without past and without future, without imagination,
without vision, without aspirations.

Wilkinson (1990)

All children experience an array of stories in the home, a
mixture of personal anecdotes, explanations, family stories,
televisual tales, traditional tales and other texts, and through
this engagement they learn a lot about story. Research evidence
suggests that the early literary experience of stories told and
written makes a significant contribution to children's later
development (Wade, 1984). Gordon Wells' (1987) longitudinal
study also found that children's early knowledge of story was
the most influential indicator of later educational achievement.

Considerable research into young children's invented stories
has been undertaken by Fox (1993). She provides clear evidence
that preliterate children with a wealth of experience of story
(gained through conversation, traditional tales, nursery rhymes,
books, television and so on) display a degree of knowledge about
narrative convention and form, and linguistic styles and plot
which is usually associated with more mature and highly literate
readers and writers.

Early years studies by Gussin Paley (1981) show how children
learn language actively through play, and the patterns of their
play reveal both their knowledge of language and their
understanding of story structure. As Moffett (1968) observed,
'Children must, for a long time, make narrative do for all.'

Different cultures and communities do make different use of
stories, Brice Heath (1983), but storytelling and thinking
through story remain a universal human competence.

So it is that we can readily conceive of ourselves as deprived
of all kinds of cultural resources, TV, theatres, even books,
but strip us of all the accumulation of stories heard and told,

reported and invented, traditional and spontaneous, and what is left of us? ...for the drive to represent experience as narrative is indestructible and catastrophe itself is after all a story we tell ourselves.

H. Rosen (1984)

In school, as well as at home, the air is thick with stories. Anecdotes and retold tales of all kinds pack the playground, the corridors, the staffroom and the classrooms. Through telling stories in these contexts, teachers and managers, administrators and support staff as well as the children make use of narrative as a way of thinking, redefining their experiences (and those of others) and giving shape and meaning to their lives.

Such tales are not often valued as part of the educational enterprise, however, and are sidelined in some classrooms as merely gossip or off-task talk. Harold Rosen (1988) argues that a narrative culture needs to be created in education which gives a central place to the *reworkings of narratives* and builds upon the oral tradition of reshaping and refashioning meaning through storytelling. In reworking and retelling personal and traditional tales in school, children can become the official storytellers, make full use of their natural powers of narrative and explore, shape and share their thoughts and feelings. In retelling traditional tales children may enter the world of fantasy and fiction, meet animals which talk, and little people with magic powers, yet the experiences of everyday living are mirrored metaphorically in these tales. As oral storytellers, the children will also be engaged in interacting with their audience and reshaping the tale through this creative social process. Children often assume their teacher wants an accurate reproduction of the tale and can become over-concerned about fulfilling this implicit demand. With time, experience and discussion, however, children come to realise that oral storytelling offers real freedom from such apparent restrictions and that retelling fosters their imaginative capacity.

The recent national revival of storytelling has made inroads into school practice, and the insightful and inspiring work of

Betty Rosen (1988, 1993) and the teachers involved in the National Oracy Project (1988–91) has further helped to raise the profile of storytelling as a traditional and accessible mode of learning. In primary education, interest in this art form is expanding rapidly as teachers find pleasure and purpose in storytelling and offer children such learning opportunities also. Teachers are discovering that narrative thought is not only supported by literature-based classrooms, but also by particular classroom contexts in which narratives are created and investigated, shaped and reshaped, shared and valued. Such learning contexts include oral storytelling, imaginative play and storydrama, and constitute the main focus of this book.

LITERACY LEARNING
THROUGH STORYTELLING

Traditional oral stories are a powerful source of inspiration in the classroom and can lead to children realising their story responses in writing, music, painting or drama. However, in becoming oral storytellers, and telling and retelling tales to different audiences, children are also developing their verbal artistry, their ability to make and shape traditional tales in their own words. These will not be empty repetitions of well-known story formulae, but imitative explorations, playful verbal experimentations which creatively revisit the narrative using the language, intonation, gesture, feeling and personal stamp of the new teller. Teachers who invite children to be storytellers enrich the classroom discourse by releasing them from the demand to recall merely for the purposes of comprehension, offering children instead the opportunity to revisit the tale and reveal their creative capacity and narrative competence. Good English practice emerges through the interdependence of the language modes of speaking and listening, reading and writing, while working in purposeful contexts and with real audiences. Storytelling can involve all four modes of communication and provide significant opportunities for learning about language and literature and developing linguistic competence.

SUPPORTING DEVELOPMENT IN
SPEAKING AND LISTENING

Oral storytelling provides a rich context for the purposeful development of speaking and listening and is a requirement in all UK primary national curricula and guidelines, both in terms of telling and retelling tales and in relation to listening to a range of tales. In the National Curriculum for English, 1995 (Speaking and listening), for example, it states that at Key Stage 1 *'Pupils should be given opportunities to talk for a range of purposes, including: telling stories, both real and imagined'*. At Key Stage 2 this statutory requirement is repeated *'including: telling and enacting stories'*. The national curricula for Scotland and Northern Ireland also state that pupils should tell and retell stories, based on, for example, memories, pictures, personal experience, literature and their imagination. Oral work is frequently less explicitly planned for in the primary curriculum as it is seen to be 'happening all the time' and often the development of speaking and listening becomes the poor relation in English practice. Work on storytelling can ensure speaking and listening is planned, integrated into the curriculum and developed in a coherent manner through collaborative group work, individual work and whole-class work.

DEVELOPING SPOKEN LANGUAGE COMPETENCE

In retelling personal and traditional stories in the classroom, children are able to develop their spoken language confidence and build on their previous experience of story. In this context they are exercising considerable power over language as they organise the structure of the tale and make spontaneous choices about vocabulary, style, language and imagery. In oral retellings, children are particularly free to embellish and exhibit their creative competence which it is often more difficult for them to demonstrate in writing. In preparing to tell a story, children are not involved in a rote-learning exercise, but in sensitively and dramatically using words to express the images, characters and events which inhabit their story. The striking language of traditional tales is usually patterned, memorable and overtly rhythmic in nature. This is the rich story language children tacitly learn to use. In the following extract from *Rumplestiltskin*, Martin and George, aged seven years, were retelling the tale on to tape. They had not heard the tale recently, but had chosen to prepare it for the school Storytelling Festival.

MARTIN   By now the Queen had forgotten all about the promises.

GEORGE   And she had the baby and she loved it, and that tiny little man came back *phoof* and he spat at her and said:

MARTIN   'I'll give you three days to guess my name and if you can't, *argh*, then I shall have your baby, *ahah! ahah! ahah!*' The Queen burst into sobs again; she was always sobbing.

GEORGE   And on the first day she said, 'Is it John?'

MARTIN   'Is it Robert?'

GEORGE   'Is it Jonathan?'

MARTIN   'Is it Paul? Is it William?'
'No, none of those names – two days left. Now, *ahah! ahah! ahah!*, I shall have your baby.'

GEORGE   So the Queen stopped sobbing and used her brain. She sent out for all the names, all the sorts of unusual names, like the Marquess of Carabess, Leonardo di Da and the Infamous One, but the nasty little man came back and said, *'No... No... No!'*

MARTIN   'No, no, no. Now I'll have your baby, oh goody goody goody, just see if I don't.'

GEORGE   That very night one of the Queen's soldiers was walking through the woods on his way home when he heard a tiny voice singing...

MARTIN   And it was singing:
The Queen, the Queen can't find my name.
I am going to have her baby.
I am going to be the King!
I am invincible! I am incredible!
I am the one and only Rumplestiltskin!

GEORGE   So the soldier ran back to the palace as fast as his feet would carry him and they woke up the Queen and he told her the nasty little man's name and when he said it, he shivered. 'Rum-ple-stiltskin, Rum-ple-stiltskin – that's his name.'

MARTIN   The Queen whispered it to herself: 'Rum-ple-stiltskin, Rum-ple-stiltskin', and... she... smiled!

In this dramatic extract from their detailed retelling of the tale, it is clear that the boys are enjoying themselves and jointly rehearsing their ability to tell the tale while simultaneously thinking forwards and remembering it. The tape is peppered with joint subvocal offerings, which prompt the turn-taking and develop the narrative action. Their text, with its apposite use of story language, its dramatic intonation, repetition and changes of pace and volume, indicates that they have a considerable implicit awareness of stories and how they work. They handle the predictable naming process with a sense of surety and speed, building the tension and threat, which is partly carried by the wicked and excited voice of Rumplestiltskin himself. This written record cannot convey the energy, commitment and experimental zeal which their voices carry, nor their affective involvement in the tale. In addition, they are clearly aware that they are telling *their* story, since when a friend asked where he could read it, Martin replied, 'I don't think we've got a copy in here, and anyway, we did our *own* one'. The tale has begun to be personalised, revisioned and reshaped by the boys, and their pleasure in the process is evident.

> ...in their oral story-telling the children are talking in a way that is fruitful for their learning. Their powers of language are being developed in a much more muscular and complex way. The imagination can operate without hindrance and hence the meanings they shape with that language are fuller and more complex.
>
> Jones (1988)

DEVELOPING ACTIVE LISTENING

As the tunes of the tale are twirled on the tongue, the storyteller shares his words and simultaneously hears these words. So there is more than one kind of active listening happening as the teller relives the tale in a creative community of listeners. As Walter Ong (1990) noted, 'Sight isolates, sound incorporates.' The imaginative qualities of listening are highlighted through regular storytelling as are children's powers of concentration. Listening to a storyteller involves interpretation and the creation of new images in the mind's eye, refashioned out of old conceptions and visualisations. It also involves getting in front of the story to anticipate the action, establish connections and make meanings. Such listening comprehension skills develop reading comprehension skills.

> It is my view that the dynamic of listening to a story being told somehow amalgamates the two processes of receiving and reflecting upon the material. Story-hearing cannot be a solitary matter, however; it is essentially and literally communal.
>
> B. Rosen (1988)

A commitment to regular storytelling therefore ensures children are given opportunities to actively listen and respond to a range of stories told by different people, as well as to tell and retell stories themselves. Traditional tales were originally intended to be listened to, and offer children the chance to become familiar with the rhythms and structure, cadence and conventions of told tales. Child storytellers, like adult tale tellers, play with the devices of the oral tradition of metre, rhythm, rhyme and repetition, and experiment with tones of voice and the rhythms of words as well as the ideas, issues and meanings in the tale. This opportunity to explore the latent possibilities in the human voice, its inflection, emphasis, cadence and the use of pause, is a useful one and through tape recordings and conferencing these aspects can be highlighted, and children's speaking and listening enhanced. In listening to such stories, children are learning to hear the colour, the drama and the emotive engagement in the sounds that words and language offer.

SUPPORTING BILINGUAL LEARNERS

Bilingual learners need the opportunity to hear, to tell and retell stories in their chosen language and need to be sure their culture and language are respected and valued in the classroom. Storytelling provides a genuine and valid opportunity to raise the status of different languages and cultures in schooling.

Pupils from minority groups may develop confidence and self-esteem through oral storytelling and through sharing their oral traditions. Parents and members of the local community may also be prepared to share their stories. In addition, the wealth of opportunities (both formal and informal) for retelling tales, and exploring stories through role-play and drama, invites the use of more than one language and the sharing of diverse cultural experience and knowledge.

Traditional stories with repeating sequences and a clear storyline offer considerable support to children who are inexperienced users of English, and can introduce them to the rhythm and sounds, grammatical structure and vocabulary of their second language. Storytelling is an effective tool to use with second-language learners since the gestures, facial expressions and body movements of the storyteller offer additional layers of meaning and facilitate understanding.

DEVELOPING KNOWLEDGE ABOUT SPOKEN LANGUAGE

In focusing upon traditional storytelling, children are able to enhance their knowledge about language, and awareness of some of the characteristic features of this genre. Children need to become versatile speakers who can choose from a variety of registers and communicate effectively. Some of these varieties are acquired as part of growing up in the local community, but others need to be the subject of conscious attention at school.

Telling stories enables such attention to be focused upon the spoken word, and the issue of standard and non-standard English may also be raised through observation and discussion of the 'voices' used by storytellers. As Chapter 3 details, through drafting, conferencing and in storytelling partnerships children can develop an understanding of the ways in which spoken language works.

> Learning to tell stories also encourages the development of a range of voices, registers, accents and dialects which can be used to effect in the telling, and the acquisition of a body of knowledge about stories – their content, their ways of representing human beings and their lives, their organisation and sequencing.
>
> Howe and Johnson (1992)

How language varies according to context and purpose can be investigated by retelling the same tale to different audiences, and the similarities and differences between oral and written versions of the same story can be studied, as can the use of a storyteller's voice and the effects which can be achieved through it. Children can enrich their communication skills through regular experience of storytelling, more confidently coming to use paralinguistic features (gestures, facial expressions) as well as linguistic features (use of tense, hyperbole, linking devices).

DEVELOPING A SENSE OF AUDIENCE

Storytelling is a demanding social process, an interactive event, since the audience makes subtle responses to aspects of the tale and this affects the tale as it unfolds. Children can develop a sense of audience too. 'I could see they were really scared of the wild woman so I made her a bit less frightening and dropped the cackle,' Anupa commented after an early years performance. The teller and told journey together in the world of story, creating socially shared meanings. Although the bond between them is temporary, it is both powerful and evocative, drawing out the linguistic and imaginative potential of all involved. The significance of storytelling lies in the experience of telling. When children retell traditional tales they become more aware of the power of their words and realise their control over their language and audience. Although potentially an empowering process, storytellers need extended opportunities to build their confidence and to develop their self-esteem. (Some children initially tell their tales to the floor and need support and encouragement to look up.)

Through practice and experience, however, children can learn to entice their audience into their tales, perhaps through conversational connections which build bridges into the world of story. For example, Hannah, aged eight years, started her tale of *The Blind Beggar* by leaning forward towards her audience of six-year-olds and asking, 'Have you ever been ill? I mean, really ill?' When they had shared their memories with her and each other, she took the lead again and pronounced, 'Well, the boy in my story gets ill too, really ill, like some of you. Let me tell you what happened...' This device linked their personal stories to her fictional one and created an appropriate social context in which her storytelling emerged as an extension of this intimate conversation. This strategy had not been planned deliberately but was instinctively employed.

Depa, aged eight years also, in telling a story to a group of her peers, introduced her central character by relating each of her heroine's character traits to friends in the assembled audience. 'She was as kind as Lizzie, as happy as Helen and played as many jokes on people as Damian, that sort of person, you know...' This metanarrative aside represented a shared piece of knowledge which served to build a bond between Depa and her audience and probably enabled more empathetic listening to occur. Sharing both personal and traditional tales in the classroom creates a rapport between individuals, draws children and adults together and helps to build a strong sense of community, as Zipes (1996) has shown.

SUPPORTING DEVELOPMENT IN WRITING

Too often, children are expected to write stories in school before they have had the opportunity to articulate their narrative in easy spoken words. In telling their tale they are able to make the story, and their response to it, their own. Producing a written retelling which builds on their oral retelling of the teacher's tale encourages children to become aware of the multiple choices available to them as storytellers and as writers, and helps them to see how they can change the world of story through changing words alone. After first hearing the tale and then retelling it, in the mind and orally, the physical act of writing becomes either a way of recording, compressing and distilling the story or an opportunity to explore and reshape it still further. In either case, perhaps part of the 'real' writing has already been undertaken in the oral process of retelling.

DEVELOPING KNOWLEDGE OF STORY STRUCTURE

The current emphasis on the ability to structure writing (NC 1995) is well supported by stories that are heard, reflected upon and retold orally. Rich experience of the folk-tale genre, and the opportunity to experience the tale through retelling it, provides children with a working knowledge of the overt structure of traditional tales.

> Users cannot produce or decipher stories without some implicit competence in respect of narrative structure... This competence is acquired by extensive practice in reading and telling stories.
>
> Rimmon-Kenan (1983)

This closeness to the shape of folk tales prompts a wide range of structural reproductions in written form. In story writing children use narrative patterns that they are familiar with, so a storytelling focus can enable learners to draw gradually upon the conventions of the folk genre, and use, for example, conventional timeless beginnings, or the problem–resolution story structure. In producing written retellings of told tales, children lean on aspects of plot, character, setting and theme in the 'original' tale. Their creative potential is therefore able to be harnessed as some of the literary conventions of story are already provided, and they are able to focus more explicitly on an imaginative re-creation. Figurative language, phrases and repetitive refrains from tales are tacitly transferred into children's writing over time, both in their narrative retellings and in other forms of writing. Changing tales into poetry builds on the repeated phrases or language patterns in tales, is an accessible way to alter the genre, and also helps children to become more conscious of language form and rhythm.

Betty Rosen (1988) observed that her pupils' poetry was influenced by the spontaneous rhythms of storytelling and prompted the children's natural rhythmic competence to surface. Certainly, oral stories, like poetry, depend on being brought to life through the power and music of the spoken word and cadence.

DEVELOPING CREATIVITY IN WRITING

The experience of living through the storytelling fosters insight and innovation and certainly enhances children's creative written competence. For example, in one class the story of *Sun Frog and Moon Frog* had been told; a story about two frog companions who sit on their lily pads all day, jumping and blinking and licking the air for flies. The Rikki Tikki Bird visits their happy abode to warn them of impending floods, but they perceive no danger and refuse to leave. Later, a storm brews up and the valiant bird returns to offer help. The frogs leap on to the bird's back and are carried three times around the world until the bird finds them a new home. The six- and seven-year-olds who had joined in the repetitive language and ritual actions in the tale had also created the storm through voice play and body percussion. After a brief class discussion, pairs of children retold the tale. Then a whole-class retelling (with new words and actions suggested by the children) completed the session.

Some weeks later, in a writing workshop, Matthew, aged seven, produced this written retelling unaided (only his spellings have been altered).

> One day Sun Frog and Moon Frog found a spaceship on the pond and fixed it up. The next day they asked some of their friends, Rat and Mole and Newt, to come with them and then they took off into space. They were flying higher and higher. Soon they were on Neptune. Then there was an enormous electric storm. Rat said, 'But there are no storms in space. This calls for International Rescue.' International Rescue were on a mission, so Sun Frog said to Moon Frog, 'Let's call the Tikki Bird and Captain Kirk and Mr Spock and Solo.' They all came to the rescue and the great Tikki Bird saved the day, and they all said, 'Hooray for the Rikki Tikki Bird. Hooray! Hooray! And he took them all home and they were safe. Hooray! Hooray!'

Matthew has used the story shape and characters from the original story, but has also drawn on characters known to him from other stories, including *The Wind in the Willows*, *Thunderbirds* and *Star Trek*. He has woven these intertextual references seamlessly into his narrative, yet ultimately allowed the mythical Rikki Tikki Bird the fairy godmother's role. This was a remarkably coherent, imaginative and well-structured piece of writing for Matthew. He has built on the accessible folk-tale structure and felt sufficiently confident to play with the tale. In composing his written narrative, he has drawn on the 'original' tale as well as other tales well known to him, to nourish and enrich his own innovative retelling. In particular, his repetitive celebration at the end of the tale is reminiscent in style of the communal repetitions he had joined in with in the class retelling. Many story writers like Matthew borrow such features from the oral tradition.

It is clear that when children come to write they make use of previous experiences with similar texts to compose new ones.

CHAPTER 2

However, teachers often read relatively long stories aloud to the class, while expecting short stories to be written. Traditional tales with their clear structure, short-story format, vivid language, cultural diversity and common archetypal themes offer quality material for supporting imaginative writing and integrating talking and writing in learning.

SUPPORTING DEVELOPMENT IN READING

In relation to reading, a focus on storytelling certainly fosters children's interest in traditional tales, tales with particular themes, cultures or characters (such as Ananse the Spider Man, or Brer Rabbit the Trickster). The National Curriculum for English (1995) states that the literature read should include *'retellings of traditional folk and fairy stories'* and *'stories and poems from a range of cultures'* at Key Stage 1 and *'myths, legends and traditional stories'* as well as *'texts drawn from a variety of cultures and traditions'* at Key Stage 2. This breadth of reading material is also expected in the Scottish and Northern Ireland guidelines and curricula. A focus on storytelling will help to ensure that this range of texts is read, reflected upon, discussed, developed and challenged.

EXTENDING THE LITERATURE AVAILABLE

In searching for stories to tell, children are prompted to dip into anthologies and to widen the range of their emotional, moral and cultural responses to texts. A brief selection of quality collections, picture-book retellings and audio cassettes available is provided in Appendix 1 (see pages 165–79).

In the last decade educationalists have come to understand much more about the ways in which 'texts teach what readers learn', Meek (1988), and how quality literature offers children a rich diet of pleasure, play and learning. Traditional tales have been refined and reshaped from powerful ingredients and still retain their imaginative essence, their ability to move, excite, fascinate and enthral the reader or listener. They also build on children's oral language experience of rhythm, rhyme and story.

PRIMARY
PROFESSIONAL BOOKSHELF
48

Traditional tales and modern retellings also provide insights into life in different cultural communities and can therefore make a significant contribution to the reading material in classrooms. The SCAA (1995) survey which examined the range of literature read in *One week in March* raised serious concerns that 'little reading of texts from other cultures and traditions was recorded'. If traditional storytelling had a higher profile in classroom practice then this arguably national imbalance could be addressed.

DEVELOPING RESPONSE TO ORAL AND WRITTEN LITERATURE

Storytellers naturally and intimately interpret and evaluate the tales they tell. So in working towards becoming traditional storytellers, children develop their response to literature, a critical component of all UK national curricula and guidelines and the assessment process. The word 'response' was helpfully defined in the Non-statutory Guidance (1989) which accompanied the original English National Curriculum 'Cox' document.

> Individual response to literature is fundamental to the POS for reading (eg POS 2, 6 and 10). Readers respond to the same text in different ways at different times: readers make analogies between their own lives, current issues and those represented in texts, using the text as a fictional commentary on their own experience.
>
> Non-statutory Guidance (1989)

This explanation builds on Iser's (1979) reader-response theory which argues that every individual has a different response to text because of their various real and fictional experiences. As Alwyin (1992) observes, the same is true in traditional storytelling since an audience of twenty will create and co-create twenty different stories in interaction with the story and the storyteller. The practical strategies described in Chapters 3 and 4 show how storytelling and related storydrama activities can enable children to engage actively with stories and develop their responses to these texts. However, the storyteller is positioned differently from the reader and as a consequence engages with the literature and the audience from the inside looking out as well as from the outside looking in. In the process of preparing to retell a tale, children will reflect upon the whole text, question and challenge it, and learn to summarise its main points and themes. Children may also become more aware of significant features in texts.

Sally, aged seven years, after several weeks of storytelling work involving telling, retelling, reading and listening to stories, observed: 'There are lots of stories where people disguise themselves, aren't there, Miss?' She made a collection of such tales, both traditional and contemporary, from the classroom shelves and added the titles of other stories she knew where characters behaved in a similar manner. Unsurprisingly, some weeks later, Sally's own written stories began to be inhabited by characters in various forms of disguise.

Response to literature will also involve reflection upon language, awareness of the words used, the development of meanings beyond the literal and the use of inference and deduction. Storytelling aids children's understanding of the symbolic nature of language and how it represents human thought and action. Knowledge of literary conventions is also learned through reading, analysing and evaluating texts, and through retelling tales in spoken and written form. In storytelling work, these interdependent language modes feed off each other and increase each child's store of meanings, developing the personal information and understanding, implicit knowledge and experience they bring to reading new texts.

DEVELOPING FLUENCY IN READING

The experience of storytelling can also enrich children's use and awareness of intonation and fluency in reading, making deeper meanings for themselves and others, through expression and voice flavour. Some tales are experienced almost as music, since the lyrical nature of the language provides patterns and harmonies which demand an aesthetic response from the audience. The inherent rhythms in some oral stories evoke reminiscences of the incantations and repetitions first encountered in nursery rhymes, playground rhythms, songs and television advertisements. So in telling and listening to tales, children learn to play with sounds and words, to hear their own tunes, create verbal patterns and discover new chords and harmonies of their own.

The inhabited voice of the child storyteller whose verbal energy, inflection and voice play bring an oral story to life can significantly influence the quality of that child's expressive reading aloud. It can also widen the range of inner voices which shape meanings in their silent reading. Taylor (1994) argues with regard to the teachers' read-aloud programme that it is 'repeatedly exposing and reinforcing patterns of grammar and other formal properties of language'.

An even stronger case can be made for traditional storytelling, which enables not just teachers but children to actively use, experience and repeat the grammatical constructions which are part of the literary language of some stories and the repetitive oral refrains of others.

DEVELOPING VISUAL IMAGES IN THE MIND

A storytelling focus can additionally prompt and develop readers' capabilities to predict and hypothesise, to make connections between texts (both between life and literature), to engage emotionally with stories and to create strong visual images. In a storytelling performance the teller has to work alongside the text, live inside the text, and leave gaps in the narrative through pause and gesture while painting pictures through words and actions. Writers work in similar ways and both teller and writer rely on the listener or reader to bring their own experiences into play to 'read' and 'see' the story.

The language of traditional tales and the intimacy of the context encourages particularly rich visualisations and makes clear imaginative demands. As Louise, aged nine years, commented to her teacher, having heard the tale *The Children of Wax* (see pages 56–7), 'Miss, I could see it all. It was like a film in my head, especially when he melted and they just shut that door on him. That was terrible.' Her involvement in the story no doubt influenced the image formation as did her previous experience (relayed later) of being shut in the garden once when the wind closed the back door.

Quality illustrations in contemporary picture books play a significant role in helping children to make interior visualisations, as the work of Graham (1990) and Doonan (1992) has shown, but oral stories are also a rich source for prompting visual images, which are rarely static as they are in a book and are full of feeling and affectivity from the interactive tale-telling encounter.

> ...picturing as a fundamental act of imagining by the reader necessary to make sense of what is read;
>
> Fry (1985)

Inexperienced readers do not always perceive pictures in the mind's eye, so oral stories with their powerful imaginative demands provide considerable encouragement for these learners. Reluctant readers can also benefit from listening to oral stories, since they can hear tales of considerable complexity (perhaps in instalments) which would, in print, be beyond them, and can be introduced to powerful action-packed stories, some of which they might choose to re-read for themselves.

In addition, the socially shared process of storytelling helps draw reluctant readers in, in ways that story reading cannot hope to do. Regular oral storytelling certainly needs to be added to the planned programme of 'read aloud/story sharing' in the classroom. More significantly, however, if children themselves engage fully in traditional storytelling, retelling stories, reading stories and writing stories this will help them to develop the considerable knowledge about language and story structure which they need to become independent and reflective readers.

STORYDRAMA, STORYTELLING
AND LANGUAGE LEARNING

Traditional stories provide rich material for investigation through drama, which in turn provides the context and conventions which shape the exploration. Using tales to step into the world of drama, however, does not involve re-enacting the story but learning about the morals, themes, characters and issues in the tale through joint discovery and imagined experience. In storydrama, through using a range of techniques, children are able to evaluate the choices and dilemmas which beset characters in traditional tales, develop insights into different points of view and make use of a wide range of speaking and listening skills in various situations. Time spent on early dramatic play is significant in developing children's imaginative and creative competence, as Gussin Paley (1981) has shown. The puppet, too, is a potent tool, capable of stimulating the imagination and bridging the gap for young children between telling tales of personal experience and retelling and making traditional tales.

LEARNING ABOUT LIVING THROUGH DRAMA

Through standing within stories and in creating new tales in drama out of the seeds of the old, children not only practise and develop a more fluent use of language but also rehearse possibilities for their own responsibilities and values. Children stand both within and outside themselves in these imaginative contexts and try on others' lives for size through the symbolic potential of drama.

> To see drama, therefore, merely as a method of stimulating environments for talk, as the descriptions in the National Curriculum orders tend to, would be to ignore its power as an immediate and accessible symbolic form which young people can use together to represent, try out, interrogate and express key areas of human experience.
>
> Neelands (1992)

Storydrama and traditional storytelling complement and enrich each other, enabling the child to symbolise, to capture and understand abstract meanings and to build a bridge between feeling and knowing. Stories investigated through active storydrama and in role-play can help children to understand a wider range of feelings and relationships through the vicarious experience of others. Folk tales, fairy tales, myths and legends represent some of the most successful material for storydrama as their archetypal concerns resonate in contemporary literature and daily living.

WORKING AT THE INTERFACE BETWEEN DRAMA, READING AND WRITING

Storydrama enables children to think in the narrative mode and helps them to consciously consider narrative as a means of interpreting and articulating experience. Further, the dramatic speculation and improvisation so central to storydrama nurtures the predictive and hypothetical nature of reading and listening to stories. Through imaginative role-play and drama, children are able to examine and explore the possibilities of what they have experienced, heard or read. Inhabiting literature in this experimental and creative fashion enables young learners to be engaged in the liberating experience of story making and active storytelling. As the storyteller Rob Parkinson (1996) has observed, 'The 'story maker' and the 'storyteller' inside us are very close cousins, maybe even siamese twins.'

As Chapter 4 details, during storydrama children plan and shape a new story, incorporate each other's oral stories about the characters into the changing structure, and challenge, question and interpret the layers of these stories in their search for meaning. In storydrama children individually and collectively interrogate, confront and transform the text. In this way new texts and tales are co-authored during the drama, aspects of which can be recorded in written form, providing a real purpose and audience for their writing. Such writing may represent different views at different moments of consciousness in the drama and provide insights into characters' inner emotions.

DEVELOPING THE IMAGINATION THROUGH STORYDRAMA

Storydrama, literature and storytelling work together to expand the imagination and create alternative worlds through image, metaphor, situation and story. Indeed, drama and language share the process of developing the imagination through role-play in these worlds, so that in the secondary years it is possible to describe the imagination as 'make-believe play without the action' (Vygotsky, 1978). All storydrama requires children to engage in active make-believe, to exercise their imagination and to speculate, modify and transform their understandings. The drama techniques employed facilitate and empower children to investigate the imaginative possibilities in the tale and to create these in words, actions and symbols. The consequences of their creations and decisions are then examined through the drama. So narrative in role-play, drama and storytelling helps to define the boundaries between reality and fantasy, while at the same time imaginatively examining the metaphoric links between them.

> ...imagination is the creation of possible realities, including the reality we actually inhabit.
>
> Smith (1992)

Investigating stories in storydrama, in role-play and with puppets can enrich these 'possible realities' through the construction of affective, powerful and imaginary story worlds.

So through stories told, created in role, read and written down, children search for their stories in the stories of others, and organise and reflect upon their personal and imaginary pasts. Significant literacy learning can take place through storytelling in all its guises if integrated language practices are designed which revolve around this traditional tool for learning.

THE CHILDREN OF WAX
An African tale

It wasn't in my time and it wasn't in your time, but it was in someone else's time that, nestled beneath the Matopos hills in Africa, there lived a family whose children were made entirely of wax. The mother and father were distraught when they realised that their children were not like others, who were made from flesh and blood. They couldn't understand it. Why had they been picked upon like this? One wax child was enough, but two, three, four children of wax?

Their mother wept and wondered, but she loved them in her heart and came to care for them as all mothers do for their children. Their father loved them too, and built them a dark wooden hut in which they could live. There they stayed, safe inside during the time of sunlight until the twilight hour descended and the heat from the sun's rays could harm them no more. The children therefore slept most of the day and came out to work at night, taking the cattle to the watering holes, tending the crops and cleaning out the compound, much as the flesh children did during the daytime.

Their hut had no windows, so the sun could not penetrate the gloom, although the youngest child, Ngwabi, had scratched and scraped a tiny chink in one wall through which he was able to peer when the sun was at certain positions in the sky. Ngwabi loved to listen to the laughter and voices of the children outside and to catch occasional glimpses of them as they played in the sunlight. His dreams were full of possibilities and imaginings. Unlike his brothers and sisters who accepted that they would never know what the world was like, Ngwabi longed to see the world. At night he would stare into the distance, searching the silhouettes of the hills with his eyes, wondering what lay beyond them. He saw the paths leading this way and that, but could never follow them, for this was far too dangerous at night-time.

He shared his thoughts with his brothers and sisters, speaking to them of his dreams and his desire for freedom.

'We are imprisoned in this hut by day and in a shroud of darkness by night,' he complained. 'We do not know what the world is really like.'

However, his siblings recognised that there were advantages to being wax children, for such children knew no pain and they were duteous sons and daughters who could work twice as hard as a child of flesh for they would never tire. But poor Ngwabi continued to dream. He began to withdraw into himself and his world of silent possibilities. His desire deepened; his frustration increased. He could think of nothing else. One day, unable to restrain his longing any further, he rushed out of their hut, out into the world, out into the light, out into the glaring temperatures of the midday sun.

Of course he could not last long out there in the searing heat and as his body began to melt, he cried out to his family to save him. His brothers and sisters heard his dying cries, but cruelly could do nothing to help him. They were even forced to close the door of the hut against him as the sun's rays scorched in towards them. All strength drained from Ngwabi and soon he was just a pool of melted wax, a liquid mass in the blazing sunshine.

When night fell, the children left their hut and gathered around the now hardening wax which had been their young brother Ngwabi. His eldest sister carefully scooped up the wax and they walked solemnly to their special place, where many a time the four of them had sat together, talked and told stories. Then in silence, Ngwabi's sister fashioned a great bird out of the wax. For feathers, they each pressed leaves from the trees into this wax bird. The leaves would protect the wax from the heat of the sun. It was a magnificent creature – its head proud, its eyes inquisitive, its feet firm.

The children took the bird to their parents and told them what had happened. Their mother took the bird in her hands and wept as she kissed Ngwabi goodbye. Their father, too, kissed it tenderly as he held the bird close to his chest. The wax children did not work that night, but placed the great bird on a rock that stood before their hut. Then they joined hands and sat around it together in silent tribute and communion.

As dawn broke, the children returned to their hut and crowded together around the small hole in the wall that Ngwabi had made. Their eyes watched and wondered. As light seeped up over the hills, it seemed as if the bird drew breath and took energy from the sun. Its wing-tips moved, stretched and fluttered. Its head turned as it looked searchingly around. Slowly and gracefully, the great bird which they had created took off up into the air. As it disappeared from their sight overhead, they could hear its wings beating. It circled their hut three times and then took off in the direction of the hills. Ngwabi, their brother, was free at last.

DEVELOPING TRADITIONAL STORYTELLING

Opportunities need to be provided in the classroom for traditional stories to be read and written, shared and responded to as well as told and retold by the children. This will enable learners to develop an openness to the multitude of meanings, images, emotions and connections that traditional tales evoke. It will prompt children to make and shape their own meanings, to internalise the structure and sequence in stories, and to enhance their linguistic competence in the process. As Harold Rosen has long argued:

> ...the human disposition to narratize experience... suggest[s] that narrative in school is not something to be *consumed* (in written form) but something to be *made* by every person in every possible way, and that it is limitless in its possibilities.
>
> H. Rosen (1988)

This chapter and the following one on drama and role-play both explore some of these possibilities, and investigate a range of creative practices which can emerge through developing storytelling in the classroom. Through nurturing oral stories and taking traditional tales as a focus, the teacher is able to release children's language potential in a myriad of ways.

> I didn't realise I knew so much about folk tales. After we had done the work I sat back and realised just how much I knew. I was really proud of myself. I never did such an easy or interesting bit of work. I wish it was always so easy.
>
> Emma, aged 8 years

As Emma's comments suggest, through working on storytelling in the classroom, teachers are building upon children's natural narrative competence, which can become a significant oral bridge to literacy. The riddles, tongue-twisters, jokes and so forth which comprise non-narrative sources of children's folklore can also be accessible starting points for young storytellers, although the focus here is on narrative sources.

ESTABLISHING A STORYTELLING ETHOS

A climate which fosters storytelling will give significant space to personal tales of lived experience as well as to traditional tales. Through sharing personal stories and researching into their family's past, children can learn about themselves, their backgrounds, culture and identity. Through telling and sharing personal tales in the classroom, the commonality of human experience is highlighted, and what it means to be human is explored. This is also a fundamental feature in traditional tales, some of which children will have encountered through the media and at home and at school. Personal and traditional tales represent the resource bank for retelling which the teacher can help the class establish, share and widen.

PERSONAL TALES

Personal tales need to be recognised as part of the educational agenda; they need time to be heard and to be told to small groups of trusted friends in the context of classroom endeavour.

> A life as led is inseparable from a life as told – or, more bluntly, a life is not 'how it was' but how it is interpreted and reinterpreted, told and retold.
>
> Bruner (1988)

Classrooms need to acknowledge the centrality of narrative as a means of making sense of oneself and the world, and give children frequent opportunities to share their stories. Teachers need to be sure to share tales of personal experience also and model appropriate probing techniques to help tellers articulate and reflect upon their experiences. The anecdotes children tell help to give shape and meaning to their lives, and the stories that they hear of others' lives are vicarious experiences which inform, bridge gaps and widen cultural understanding. All too frequently, teachers demand written exposition of personal news or memories, yet the oral version of such events is often richer, relayed with verve, feeling and enthusiasm. Freed from the constraints imposed by writing, the oral narrative has considerable value for the individual and needs to be recognised for its contribution to the creation of community.

Classrooms where personal stories are told can become cohesive contexts where individuals are valued and respected. Autobiographies matter and such stories need to be heard by others, and revisited by the teller in an attempt to establish identity and self-respect. The task of retelling a personal tale involves the selection of material, the structuring and sequencing of the narrative and the shaping and sharing of it. This needs to be done in an accessible manner which will entice the listeners, engage them in the story, help them to identify with themes or characters and release them at the close of the tale. All this happens spontaneously as a tale unfolds in the intimacy of a conversational context. Children think through story and can develop their language competence and confidence through retelling personal tales.

Personal tales can be prompted in a variety of ways. These could include:

✦ teachers' personal oral stories (stories breed stories);

✦ timelines which trace major events since birth, or during one year or term;

✦ 'emotions' graphs which map out the perceived emotional highs and lows across time;

✦ photographs of past experience which trigger memories;

✦ objects and artefacts which encapsulate past occasions;

✦ literature which prompts reminiscences;

✦ work on siblings, grandparents and other relatives.

Collecting family stories can also contribute to self-esteem, build a sense of self and support a storytelling climate. Children can research their family folklore and the oral histories of their relatives. Some parents and grandparents may even be persuaded to share their stories in person, while others may be prepared to record these on to audio cassettes which have been sent home. There may also be local legends or community tales to be discovered, researched and retold, all of which can make effective bridges between tales of personal experience and traditional tales.

TRADITIONAL TALES

As well as encouraging children to share personal tales and telling their own, teachers need to make a commitment to regularly telling traditional tales from many cultures, perhaps seeking to invite other teachers, local librarians or professional storytellers to tell such tales also.

A storyteller's chair for teachers and children to use, with a cloth draped over it can give the activity status, although many informal retellings will take place elsewhere in pairs and groups. The audience do need to group around the storyteller, to help create a comfortable context, since desks or tables act as barriers between the teller and told.

Access to story tapes of traditional tales will serve to enrich provision and widen the selection for children to retell and work upon. Children can also keep their own cassette of storytelling work that they have undertaken. This might include oral drafts and role-play dialogues, as well as final retellings. Retelling is at the heart of storytelling, so plenty of opportunities need to be provided for children to tell and retell tales.

Brainstorms of the titles of known tales often reveal much about the children's understanding of the term 'traditional tales' and can also challenge the teacher's perception, as the list on page 62, compiled by a class of seven- to eight-year-olds, indicates. Generated in small groups, it was compiled in just 20 minutes and makes intriguing reading.

Batman
Beauty and the Beast
The Tortoise and the Hare
The Little Match Girl
The Sly Young Fox and the
  Little Red Hen
Babes in the Wood
Little Red Riding Hood
The Enormous Turnip
Snow White and the Seven Dwarfs
Jack and the Beanstalk
Puss in Boots
The Boy Who Cried Wolf
The Tinderbox
The Selfish Giant
The Elves and the Shoemaker
Rumplestiltskin
Pied Piper
The Little Mermaid
Robin Hood
The Three Little Pigs
King Midas
The Princess and the Pea

The Old Woman Who Lived
  in a Shoe
Tom Thumb
The Donkey Who Sneezed
The Gingerbread Man
Baba Yaga
The Wizard of Oz
The Goose that Laid the
  Golden Egg
Hansel and Gretel
The Porridge Pot
Peter and the Wolf
Cinderella
Rapunzel
The Ugly Duckling
The Sheep's Tail
Goldilocks and the Three Bears
The Wolf's Tail
The Elephant and the Six
  Blind Men
Sleeping Beauty
The Emperor's New Clothes
The Tailor's Button

Disney reproductions clearly feature in the list, as do a few contemporary films and some tales the teacher had recently shared, but the overall breadth of their corporate knowledge of folklore is encouraging and represents a rich repertoire for the class to lean on. A collection like this one could be sorted and recorded on strips of card, then classified in various ways. It could also be used to establish retelling sessions in fours, when pairs swap tales known to them, but not known or remembered by the other pair. The initial experience of retelling well-known and familiar tales may help to highlight the nature of oral storytelling and its many changing faces.

THE READING OF FOLK TALES, MYTHS AND LEGENDS

Reading a range of folk tales, myths and legends plays a central part in establishing a storytelling ethos, both tales that have derived from ancient oral traditions across the world and those that have been more recently created.

Collections of folk tales and pictorial retellings need to be readily available to support and extend children's work. Children will often turn to these to widen their bank of known stories, to read those that have been told to them or to find alternative versions or tales with similar themes. Many schools have set up boxes of traditional tales which can be booked by teachers for half a term to support their storytelling work. Resource boxes can be further supplemented by the children's written retellings edited into collections of folklore, and oral retellings edited on to story tapes with accompanying music and percussion.

GIVING TRADITIONAL TALES PHYSICAL STATUS IN THE CLASSROOM

Giving traditional tales a physical profile will contribute to the climate in the classroom, with displays, mobiles, and artwork creating evidence of the class's journeys into such stories. A directory of known traditional tales could be made to highlight and celebrate the class's corporate knowledge.

Story quilts can be constructed out of hexagon shapes made from paper or cloth. These are a visually stimulating way of summarising the children's repertoire, with the title of the tale written or initialled on the reverse and a single symbol representing the tale drawn or stitched on the cover. Additional patchwork pieces for new tales can be stapled or stitched on to the quilt over time, so that as the children add to their resource bank their class story quilt grows.

Story murals which show the setting of a tale, or the geographical and physical features common to several tales, can create a useful display. Creating board-games based on a selection of traditional tales or drawing on common characters, settings and conflicts encountered in this fictional world of folklore can also be worthwhile, encouraging children to revisit tales and notice links between them. In addition, establishing tale tellers' 'bags' which contain simple story props, puppets and artefacts, can prompt retellings at home and provide visual memory aids for children.

REMEMBERING AND LEARNING TALES

Stories are not reproduced through rote memorisation, word for word, sentence for sentence. They are retold and reborn on each occasion with a different audience and are, as Betty Rosen (1993) notes, 'for the moment, the exclusive creation of the teller'.

To help children to remember tales and be able to retell tales that are new to them, the teacher will need to focus on a range of strategies which encourage awareness of the story structure, pattern, plot, characters and theme. The suggestions noted below represent different ways of remembering stories (these are extended in Chapter 6). All storytellers need to develop story memory, an understanding of story structure from which they can work. This structural insight and sense of knowing the tale may be achieved through a range of framework activities which seek to categorise and visualise story features and events. This might include using any of the following strategies.

STORYBOARDS

Storyboards can reinforce the sequence of events in a tale and enable the teller to retain six strong but simple visual images around which the oral story can be retold. On paper folded to create six boxes this picture summary provides both structure and sequence to the narrative and can act as a memory prompt.

THREE SEEDS OF STORY

Three seeds of story can be made, dividing the story into a beginning, a middle and an end. Three paper cut-outs of seeds can be illustrated with simple numbered pictures or written summaries from the tale. The middle seed may need to be larger than the others to reflect the structure of the tale. Once the young storytellers have these seeds in their hands, then each section of the story can grow, watered by their words in the retelling. With early years children, an extension of this activity is to make paper flower pots to plant the three story seeds in.

When children have grasped this concept, they will refer to the three imaginary 'seeds of story' in story conferences and discussions. Older children can use the same strategy to identify three essential components in the tale, and the issues which it seeks to explore.

STORY PLATES

Story plates are a useful visual tool for helping children to record the story structure and the sequence of main events in the tale that they have chosen for retelling. This idea builds upon the old Chinese tale *The Willow Pattern*, which has been summarised as a story picture on china plates and tableware known as the willow-pattern design.

In this love story about class and family duty, Koong Shee and her impoverished lover Chang are eventually transformed into immortal doves who live for ever above the landscape which represents their story's journey.

A willow-pattern plate

After telling this tale and showing the children a willow-pattern plate and its design, the teacher can challenge them to create an alternative story-plate design to fit their chosen tale on a paper plate.

This visual aid can act not only as an ordered reminder of the tale but also as a 'security blanket' for retelling. Barry, aged eight, refused to join the storytelling afternoon without his paper plate, yet never once glanced at it during his retelling of *The Wolf's Tail*. It provided him with the knowledge that should he forget part of the story the plate would prompt his memory, and the construction of it had helped embed the pattern of the tale in his story memory.

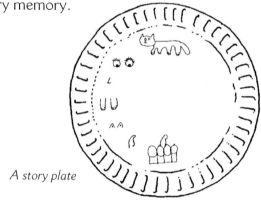

A story plate

KEYWORD SUMMARIES

Keyword summaries can be created and listed in sequence to act as triggers to the various parts of the tale. These lists can also be divided into beginning, middle and end, if the storyline is linear enough.

Matthew, aged nine, wrote this keyword summary to support his retelling of *How the Crab got its Back*. This strategy is particularly helpful for storytellers who are less visually oriented, and creates a backbone for the tale to which the teller adds substance in her retelling.

A keyword summary for the tale How the Crab got its Back

> Two sisters
> old woman – river
> sings? – yes
> blessing – beauty
> sister – old woman
> sings? – no
> crab

STORY MAPS

Story maps can be drawn by recording the geographical locations in the tale and plotting the central pathway taken by the protagonist or other characters. This maps out the journey of the tale, organises the story content, and is particularly useful applied to quest tales. The map depicts the path of the action, and significant words or refrains can be included. This particular activity lends itself to group work and enables children to share their understandings of the physical and structural features of the tale.

Using a poster-sized sheet of paper, some nine-year-olds drew a map showing different scenes and venues within *The Weaving of a Dream*, which took the following form:

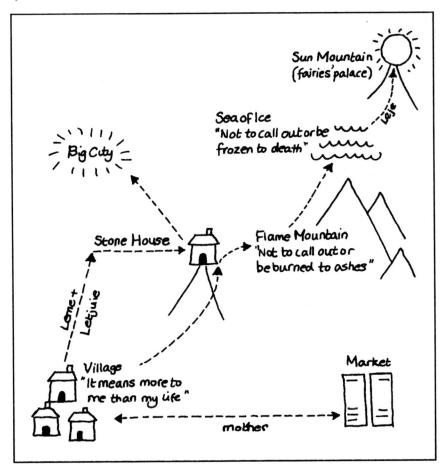

SYMBOLIC SUMMARIES

Symbolic summaries are another way of recording the structure of the tale to support recall and fix the story in the mind. These seek to avoid detailed pictures but offer implicit action through a combination of keywords, symbols, initials and so on.

Victoria, aged ten, depicted the opening section of *The End of Baba Yaga* in this almost algebraic way. The small visual symbols helped her to reconstruct the events and feelings in this section of the story in her retelling, as layers of meaning are implied in each of the ordered pictures.

A symbolic summary for the tale The End of Baba Yaga

STORY TIMELINES

Story timelines can also prompt discussion of the story structure and assist story memory. Each child is given a blank card on which they record (through writing or drawing) what they consider to be the most significant episode in the tale. In groups, the children place their cards in a timeline that indicates the sequence of significant events in the tale, taking additional cards to fill in less important episodes.

WORDLESS PICTURE BOOKS

Wordless picture books of the tale can be made to help highlight key elements and provide a clear sequence to the narrative as they offer a simple visual structure to the story. These can be constructed in many ways including folding a piece of A4 paper to create eight boxes, and then folding vertically to make a simple book. A picture in each box can be drawn of each of the key elements of the tale. However, these texts can represent a barrier between the storyteller and their audience and may be best put to one side during an oral retelling.

STORY SHAPES

Story shapes can be drawn by children to follow the journey of the tale and develop story memory. This activity focuses on how the narrative is constructed and connects with Propp's (1968) work on the structural components in folk tales. The group discussion about shapes which might represent and symbolise the story can help the children to understand the significant moves in the tale, and the accompanying visual secures it in the mind.

An example of a story shape constructed by a group of ten-year-olds on *Ladder to the Sky* is shown below.

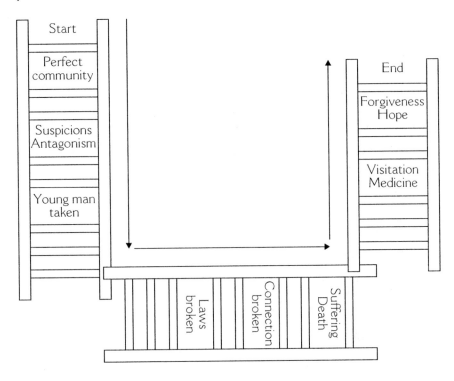

Their corporate debate about the story shape was long and heated, particularly over whether the last 'invisible ladder' should reach the sky. Their final shape attempts to reflect the ladder being descended by man, broken and later reconstructed. It works well as a metaphor for the fall and forgiveness of the human race and suggests that they grappled with the spirit of the story and made connections with other stories.

All the strategies described so far in 'Remembering and learning tales' have sought to enable children to analyse the construction of the narrative, to recall the overall sequence of events and to become well acquainted with the tale. This builds their confidence in the story in preparation for retelling, and enables the storyteller to apply her creative energy to imaginatively retelling, not recalling, the tale.

Specific work can also be done on recognising the distinctive story patterns and structures of some folk tales, such as cumulative, sequential and number patterns. In learning to retell traditional tales, children develop considerable knowledge about story structure, and with this in hand they can then attend to the characters and language of the tale. Tales are not remembered as a series of structural moves alone, but as a story inhabited by living characters.

Developing an awareness of the attitudes and feelings of key characters is important and can be enhanced through the use of drama techniques as well as through retelling. Through hot seating characters and accessing their conscience in interior monologues and through tracking their thoughts, insights into individuals' motives and attitudes can be constructed. In this chapter the section on 'Investigating and experimenting with tales' (page 82) also focuses on character.

Ways of identifying the memorable language features within the tale and utilising them are explored in 'Reflecting on storytelling' (page 90). However, many of the story-shape activities examined above prompt discussion of structure, character and language and harness the children's awareness of all three components as they work on remembering the tale.

ORGANISING OPPORTUNITIES FOR RETELLING

A variety of informal opportunities to tell and retell tales offer children different audiences to interact with, and the experience of voicing the tale, living it and shaping it through the telling. Tales can also be retold in writing, but the focus of this section is on organising oral retellings in pairs and groups within the classroom. In particular, the emphasis is on only partial retelling of tales rather than always attempting a full retelling. This can provide early success and offers children an accessible often collaborative opportunity to practise retelling and develop their confidence and competence as storytellers.

IN PAIRS

Pairs can work together as storytelling partners to produce a shared collaborative retelling of a tale on tape or a live performance of their chosen tale.

To reinforce the class repertoire of known traditional tales, a 'lucky dip' can be created. All the titles from the initial brainstorm are written on cards and placed in a top hat. One child in the pair dips in and removes a card, and together they retell the tale that has been randomly selected. If the tale is unknown to both children, their role is to create a traditional tale around the given title, perhaps reading or hearing the better known version on another occasion.

Following the teacher's storytelling, pairs can also work as 'teller and listener' partners, swapping roles as the retelling progresses, so that the tale is retold by both members of the partnership. This strategy is a particular challenge for the listener, who is asked not to interrupt the storyteller, even when the story is taken in another direction or new elements are added. The listener needs to accept these as 'given' and build on them when the teacher indicates, perhaps with a chime bar or tambourine, that it is time to swap roles.

Additionally, the teacher can divide the class into two halves, A and B, and then tell each half of the class a different short story. Then children from each group form A and B pairs to exchange the stories that they have heard. Providing time for the separate groups to practise their tale before the pairs exchange their stories is worthwhile; in fact, the children may wish to work on the structure of the tale to develop their story memory prior to retelling it.

A variation on this theme is the teacher telling the first part of a tale to half the class and the remainder to the rest of the class, informing the class which half of the tale they have heard. Pairs then form to tell the whole story. This strategy of fusing the two halves of the tale together prompts considerable discussion about various characters and events within the tale and develops a listening ear and a need to know, but it only suits some tales. *How the Crab got its Back* is possible to use in this way (see pages 128–9). The second part could start with the haughty Yolanda not listening to her sister and rushing down to the river in search of riches.

Time for each group to dwell on the possible elements of the unknown section is vital and draws on their knowledge of narrative structure and the features inherent within traditional folk tales. This time for prediction encourages focused listening when their partners retell their part of the story. Time can also be set aside for children to prepare their part and to discuss performance features, the memorable language components and the beginning or ending of the tale.

In addition, pairs can be asked to select a memory from the story they have just heard, to 'freeze' it as a visual image in their minds and share it with their story partner. In this instance each child retells only a section of the tale, starting just before and finishing just after the frozen memory or visual picture. This reduces the length of the task, avoids the driving power of the plot, and encourages the children to focus upon a detailed retelling of one section of the tale. It also enables the storytellers to concentrate on the characters, the atmosphere or its themes in more detail, to inhabit the visual picture they see and to 'dig down' into that section of the tale.

IN GROUPS

Group retellings can be prompted by making and using story dice. These dice have different story symbols from the group's repertoire of known tales drawn upon each face. Initially children take it in turns to throw a number dice, and when a six is thrown the child must throw the story dice and retell an extract from the tale depicted on the uppermost face of the story dice.

In one group of seven-year-olds a story dice was made with the following simple symbols from stories depicted on different faces: a shoe and a wand from *Cinderella*; the spinning wheel, flax and gold from *Rumplestiltskin*; the cow on the roof from *Gone is Gone*; the hats of the seven dwarfs from *Snow White*; the bridge and three pairs of horns from *The Three Billy Goats Gruff*; and a gingerbread man and the river from *The Gingerbread Man*. The group threw the number dice in turn and when one child threw a six, that child also threw the story dice and found it had landed with *The Three Billy Goats Gruff* facing upwards. She then had two minutes to retell a self-selected extract from the story before the game continued.

Groups can add their own rules and conventions to this simple game which provides an opportunity to revisit and retell scenes from well-known tales. It is worthwhile encouraging children to avoid retelling from the beginning of the tale and challenging them to select a scene from the story.

Another strategy for group retelling develops from the metaphor of the three seeds of story (see page 64). The teacher may tell the beginning, middle and end of a story to three different groups of pupils. The children then join up in threes to create a story from the fusion of the story seeds. Each seed has a significant part to play in this process, which demands considerable concentration and attention to create a seamless whole.

Alternatively, the teacher may tell only part of the tale and challenge the children in groups to finish the tale. Having discussed, planned and agreed on their ending, each group can be re-formed, so that the new groups are comprised of individual children from all of the previous groups. Using a rainbow strategy to achieve this would involve giving each child in the class the name of a colour and asking all those with the same colour to sit together. Each child retells their initial group's agreed ending to the tale. This strategy highlights the many possibilities for different endings in a tale.

Additionally, groups can tape their retelling of a tale, in whatever form they wish, perhaps dividing the roles among them to cover sound effects, music, a narrator, characters and so forth, or simply retelling it in turns section by section. The tape recorder is not as demanding as a live audience and it often releases children to be more playful and experiment with voices and sound effects in a way which live performance may not.

AS A CLASS

The teacher may tell a story and ask the children to retell it together in the class story circle. In this activity the story is passed around the class, with the new storyteller taking up the tale where the last one left off. There are many ways of managing this. The children can retell a sentence each, or a significant event each, or more informally and through tacit negotiation simply share as much of the story as they wish, bearing in mind that all the children in the class need to be able to take a fair turn.

A story token can formalise the handing over of the tale, and whoever holds the symbolic token holds the 'telling ground'. The token may relate to the tale, such as a crabshell for *How the Crab got its Back*, or a section of ivy for *Ladder to the Sky*.

These large story circles are excellent vehicles for communal retelling and careful listening, for enriching simple tales with vivid description, and for developing awareness of others' needs in a story circle. Some children will only wish to offer a few words and then pass on the story token; others may wish to tell large sections of the tale, but will be conscious of the length of the complete tale and the number of tellers and will limit themselves accordingly. Small group story circles are also possible.

A snowball strategy can be used at the end of a storytelling project. Individuals select and prepare to tell one personal or short traditional story. In pairs, the children swap their stories; pairs then make fours, and only one story from each pair is shared. Fours make eights and repeat the process, sharing only two tales between them. Eights become sixteens, and again only two stories are retold. Finally, as a whole class, these stories are heard, and other volunteers can retell their tales, or tales that they have heard during the snowball. A snowball strategy is only feasible with short stories, but is useful because it engages children in clarifying the features of a good short oral story in an intuitive way. It is valuable to undertake a more explicit discussion of these features with examples from their selected tales.

All informal storytelling opportunities build children's confidence as storytellers. In retelling tales and parts of tales to their friends, to partners, their peer group and in the whole-class story circle, children experience the power and influence of the audience and gain confidence in the story, its themes and issues. Retelling liberates children to explore the tale creatively through the process of retelling it. Each teller builds on or adapts the story structure, the characters and language, and establishes the spirit of the story through revisiting it on different occasions.

Young children in particular, however, tend to worry about 'getting the story right' or 'remembering it all'. Regular retelling of tales supported by discussion can help children realise that this is not a prerequisite. Accuracy is not the issue. Affective involvement and a creative response is of far more significance, since traditional tales are constantly renewed and refreshed through the process of retelling them. Reading several alternative versions of a well-known folk tale can help children to appreciate the legitimacy of reworking and reshaping tales through retelling. Understanding this critical feature of the oral tradition is essential and is one of the many important lessons that storytelling offers learners.

DEVELOPING STORYTELLING TECHNIQUES

Working towards a specific storytelling event will provide the children with a real reason for drafting an oral story and developing the 'performance' elements of tale telling. These techniques and skills can contribute considerably to effective storytelling and are discussed in Chapter 6 in relation to teachers as storytellers. Children, too, can build upon their confidence and competence as storytellers and fluid communicators. The suggestions noted are designed to assist children who are preparing to be storytellers to a particular audience in developing their expertise and enhancing their awareness of the possible features of performance that they could choose to employ.

Prior to the event or festival, children will need to select a story to be shared. Using the class directory of tales or taped tales or written anthologies, children will need to choose a tale that they wish to retell several weeks before the event. They would be well advised to avoid universally known tales to increase the chance of the tale being new to their audience. Activities to help children remember their tale can be undertaken, and practice sessions can be provided that enable children to draft the tale on to tape and then review it with a story partner or in small groups. Practice can also be prompted in the home context, with children being encouraged to retell the tale to younger siblings, parents and grandparents.

'Paula, my little sister, won't sit still and listen when I tell her my story,' Joseph complained. 'She runs about.'

'If you get her to join in the noises and that, she'll pay more attention,' responded Mark, the voice of experience (he had two younger sisters).

Helping children to identify some of the conventions and performance features of storytelling creates a valuable target for them to work towards and provides them with a more conscious awareness of these features. However, these skills need to be seen in context, since storytellers are not actors. Listening to a professional storyteller on tape, on video or in person and asking the children what they noticed can be a useful starting point. What did the storyteller do with her body and her voice? Did she use any props? Did she do anything which seemed different or surprising which might be particular to storytelling? A second viewing or listening may help them to articulate their responses. Discussions about the various styles and traditions in storytelling across and within different cultures, countries and continents can also become a focus for study and research, celebrating similarities and exploring the diverse styles in existence.

STORYTELLING CONVENTIONS

The teacher can prompt the creation of 'features of performance' lists. By telling the same short story twice, once as well as possible and once in an obviously incompetent and uninterested fashion, the skills being used in storytelling can be highlighted. A class of seven- to eight-year-olds who had just heard two retellings of the story of *The Tailor's Button* made it clear to their teacher how they felt:

'The first one was real, exciting and made me want to listen. The other one was just boring.'

'In the last one you never looked at us, Miss. I didn't feel part of it.'

'I liked the first one best. You did more with your hands and I could see it all happen.'

The class, together with the teacher, turned their discussion into a list of storytelling conventions; not rules, but features worth considering in preparation for a live performance.

Storytellers could try to:	
look at people sometimes	make an effort
remember it or make it up	avoid going um... er... um... er...
put expression in their voice	use actions and/or sounds
give lots of details	make their face tell the story

The role of listeners was also identified by the same class. Noted below, it does seem extremely exacting, but, as young Kurt observed with conviction, 'If the story's a good one and the teller makes it real, you just imagine it and you don't need to fidget.'

<u>Story listeners could try</u>:

not to fidget or fiddle	to hear the tune in the tale
to see pictures in their mind	to sit still
not to shout out or whisper	to look at the storyteller
to listen carefully	to lose themselves in the story

Making large posters of these features gives status to the children's views and is an invaluable support and structure to use in storytelling conferences. Clearly, different features can be highlighted by the teacher and added to the list over time. However, it needs to be acknowledged that there are many ways to tell tales which vary considerably across different traditions and cultures, and children will develop their own styles and storytelling techniques through experience, discussion and reflection.

STORYTELLING CONFERENCES

Storytelling conferences in small groups can help children to discuss the layers of meaning in their chosen tale as well as identify areas for development in terms of performance or technique. Children can refine and polish their storytelling skills, their use of voice, gesture and facial expression. In a conference group one child might retell a section of a tale, the rest of the group then praising the skills which have been well demonstrated and focusing on one or two aspects where there is room for development. If the children themselves have identified the conventions they wish to observe, this opportunity to discuss voice, pace, gesture, eye contact and so on can be very valuable, particularly in the context of a small number of peers who know the story.

There has been a strong emphasis on written drafting in the last ten years, but I had always assumed that an oral story was something that emerged like a mayfly and then went away. Given supportive criticism, it seems that children are capable of 'redrafting' stories orally and indeed are keen to do so as there is less labour involved.

Jones (1988)

As Pat Jones notes, there are parallels here with redrafting writing for meaning through response partnerships and conferences. In storytelling conferences, groups often suggest gestures to go with specific characters, or actions to accompany repetitive refrains, as well as possible creative adaptations and additions. Such groups can discuss how the themes can be evoked, and provide a supportive context in which the teller can experiment with the tale and its presentation. Tony Alwyin's (1989) video entitled *Children as Storytellers* provides some illuminating evidence of the value of conferencing in this way.

FOCUSING ON SOUNDS AND WORDS

Focusing on particular aspects of storytelling can be an effective way to raise awareness of the many complex elements of performance. For example, a music class working on group sound collages for particular stories will experience the contribution that voices, instruments and body percussion can make to the development of atmosphere, tension, anticipation and a sense of place. Through taping tales and adding accompanying music, groups can be prompted to explore how sound and music create images, convey emotions and construct meanings.

Identifying memorable language from the story, which children recall and wish to include in a retelling, is also worthwhile. This might include noting the obvious repetitive refrains, particularly rich language or powerful words and lyrical phrases in the tale. Such language patterns provide the story with an overall flavour, a sense of sound and feeling.

> Each story has its own sound. If the storyteller is not
> sensitive to that sound, I feel that the special aura that story
> radiates will be lost... there are word sounds that may not
> belong to that story and there will definitely be word sounds
> that do.
>
> Barton (1986)

There are sounds and rhythms, as Bob Barton observes, that fit harmoniously into particular tales, but would create discord in other stories. This feel for the savour and flavour in language and conscious awareness of the difference between more and less appropriate story language develops gradually over time, through hearing oral stories, telling and retelling them and discussing this aspect of storytelling.

William, aged eight, commenting on *The Children of Wax* noted, 'It was like a lullaby really. It didn't send me to sleep, but it sounded like one, don't you think?'

Various intonation patterns and volumes of voice can be tried and experimented with to help children to make informed choices and selections about words and their sounds and rhythms. Such a focus on language will inevitably prompt consideration of voice play and verbal variety, enabling children to become more aware of both the words chosen and the way in which they are communicated.

FACIAL EXPRESSION AND GESTURE

When children are working towards becoming experts in this art form, for a school storytelling festival or a book week for example, then it is worthwhile working explicitly on other optional elements of performance, including facial expression, gesture, visual aids and artefacts.

In working on facial expression and gesture it will be important to stress that all gestures are optional. However, children's natural use of gesture and body movement can be enhanced, and their paralinguistic repertoire widened, if the conference discussions focus on these features. The teacher can also tell the class part of a tale without such features and then ask for their advice. What kinds of actions would be appropriate? At what points in the tale? What additional meanings could they convey? The flavour and spirit of the tale can be enriched by such features of performance, which some children will adopt very easily while others will need the confidence, time and experience to use effectively.

DEVELOPING A SENSE OF OCCASION

Children's awareness of audience and their ability to involve their listeners develops through experience. Does the story that they have chosen to tell lend itself to overt audience participation? The more subtly interactive nature of storytelling can be reflected upon during conferences and their experience of how audiences alter the tale shared.

To give their tale telling a sense of occasion, they may like to establish a ritual such as the opening of a miniature story chest, the 'lighting' of the story fire or the use of a conventional timeless 'starter'. In Chapter 6 a variety of traditional beginnings and endings are listed. Children can use these or begin with the ritual Caribbean 'Cric' to which the audience respond 'Crac' as a way into their tale. Children delight in creating their own ritual phrases for opening and closing the class storytelling time and finding words in which they can wrap up their own retelling.

'Our story blanket will keep these tales warm until we tell them again,' Hannah suggested, and this became one class's ritual phrase for closing their storytelling session, which involved 'laying' their tales on a real story blanket that was folded and put away until the next 'tell a story time'.

The ability to share stories by word of mouth may be universal, but the confidence to do so can be sensitively enhanced. Styles can be experimented with and techniques explored for their possible application. Helping children to 'play with' tales highlights the artistic nature of storytelling, the oral making, shaping and sharing.

INVESTIGATING AND EXPERIMENTING WITH TALES

Traditional tales are constantly born again in the mouth of the teller or redrafted at the end of a pen. Storytellers naturally experiment with tales and play with the characters, the themes and the language in the story to create new meanings through subtle alterations. Changes in retellings, whether unconscious adaptations or deliberate planned differences, can be fostered and validated by investigative activities which highlight the endless possibilities for 'revisioning' – a term used by Betty Rosen (1988). Such work can help children understand how folk tales have been altered over time, as they were retold by different tellers to different listeners, and rewritten by different writers for different audiences. Revisioning also gives children ownership over their own creative retelling.

> Retelling provides growing writers with the secure framework of events and plot, and frees them to work on developing awareness of landscape, character, dialogue and imaginative reflection...
>
> Foggin (1992)

An identical argument can be applied to oral retelling. In this context children do not have to concentrate on inventing the basic components of the tale and are free to allow their imagination to consider alternatives, adjustments and transformations. The creative reworking of the tale is uniquely theirs, germinated in the earth of the 'original'.

> I feel I'm in charge when I tell stories. I can make it go the way I want and that's exciting.
>
> Darren, aged 9 years

Particular attention may need to be given to encouraging children's creative and experimental retellings as there is a tendency for many learners to assume that accurate reproduction is what their teacher requires. Liberating children from this implicit demand can be empowering and enable them to feel in control, as Darren acknowledges.

INVESTIGATING THE NATURE OF TRADITIONAL TALES

A range of practical strategies can be employed to investigate traditional tales and make explicit some of the multitude of alternative retellings which exist. Initially it may be helpful to focus on the very well-known folk tales, myths and legends to help children make more conscious their knowledge about these tales and transfer this understanding and insight to the new tales which they hear and read. Some of the activities which could be undertaken to investigate the nature of traditional tales include:

✧ identifying the typical ingredients which make up traditional tales (simple repetitive plots, supernatural elements, fantastic events, magic, the numbers 3 and 7, tasks to perform);

✧ identifying the typical characters who inhabit traditional tales (princes, princesses, kings, queens, stepmothers, fairies, wolves, dragons, witches, frogs);

✧ exploring notions of heroes and heroines (looking at expectations of behaviour, physical appearance and attitude);

✧ examining alternative written versions of the same tale;

✧ examining sexism in traditional tales;

✧ examining traditional beginnings and endings;

✧ identifying messages and themes found in traditional tales;

✧ examining several traditional tales against a typical pattern.

A simplified version of Propp's (1968) structural analysis of folk tales may help with the last activity noted above:

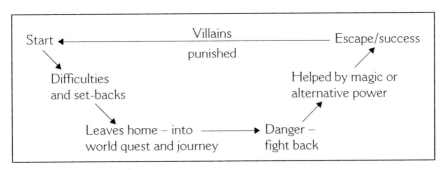

The many parallels that exist across the various forms of traditional folklore provide a sound basis to work from, as new tales to investigate are told by teachers and retold and revisioned by children. The English Centre's publications *Making Stories* and *Changing Stories* raise a number of questions concerning gender, character and the construction of folk tales, and are useful classroom resources for investigating such stories.

CHANGING STORIES

As well as the numerous minor alterations which oral retelling inevitably involves, there are a range of other changes which retellers can choose to make. A selection of options are listed below, many of which lend themselves more easily to written retellings but can also be employed as oral adaptations.

Changing stories in these ways is worth working upon explicitly in the classroom, and enables children to create their own versions and to examine the consequences of single alterations while still building on the broad base of the tale. These include:

✧ replacing the tale in a different geographical setting or historical period;

✧ changing the ending or providing more than one alternative ending;

✧ changing the style or tone of the telling;

✧ creating an earlier episode which leads into the tale;

✧ creating a follow-up tale which draws on surviving characters;

✧ adding a magical dimension to the tale;

✧ changing one character's behaviour and attitudes in the tale;

✧ changing the genre by turning the tale into a poem, a news article, playscript or local legend.

> The changes which a reteller might make look a bit cold blooded when listed... yet such changes may be most subtle, intricate, ingenious and full of feeling in the event.
>
> B. Rosen (1993)

Professional writers as well as oral storytellers have trodden this road of revisioning for centuries, changing, exchanging, reducing, expanding, altering and experimenting with traditional tales. Children need access to these retellings as models for their own work and to legitimise this creative endeavour.

Fiona French's *Snow White in New York*, Jan Sciescka and Lane Smith's *The Stinky Cheeseman and other Fairly Stupid Fairy Tales* and examples of Tony Ross's clever retellings, such as *Stone Soup*, provide excellent exemplar material in this genre of reworked tales. Through the experience of reading altered versions and the opportunity to experiment with their own retellings, children's creative confidence grows and they become more aware of the linguistic choices and alternative options available to both writers and storytellers.

INVESTIGATING CHARACTERS

Investigating and experimenting with characters within traditional tales can help children to develop empathy and a clearer understanding of motive and behaviour. Drama is an invaluable tool to use in this regard. Through metaphorically wearing the character's shoes in different situations children can develop an insider's view and a personal perspective upon the action. Chapter 4 offers strategies for studying character through storydrama and puppetry.

Gender issues can also be explored through working on characters. Reading some of the forgotten folk tales which retain strong roles for women can help to redress the gender balance and prompt discussion of the portrayal of characters in tales. Alison Lurie's *Clever Gretchen* and Jay William's *The Practical Princess* represent useful literature to support this work and provide alternative role models for men and women. Discussing or challenging the character stereotyping found in some tales, whether of men and women, wolves, beasts, witches or stepmothers, can encourage children to avoid thinking of people or animals in generalised ways based on very limited information.

In addition, prior to hearing a tale, lists of descriptive words and phrases can be drawn up to describe an unknown character, for example the heroine Vasseila in the Russian tale *The End of Baba Yaga*. Following the telling of the tale, a comparison between the character stereotypes predicted and the retold reality can be drawn.

Drama techniques such as hot seating, role-play, thought lines and interior monologues can help children to develop a more detailed perception of character, with real values and attitudes rather than a set of gender stereotypes. However, the following activities can contribute to a richer understanding of characters' motives and behaviour.

CHARACTER MAPS

A character map or sociogram can be drawn to focus upon relationships between characters. Groups select a central character and place the remainder of the cast in positions around this person, with brief statements or words indicating the nature of their relationship and perceptions of each other. This sociogram of the young man in *Ladder to the Sky* (see pages 11–12) was created by a group of nine- and ten-year-olds. Their final diagram represented a compromise between their various views.

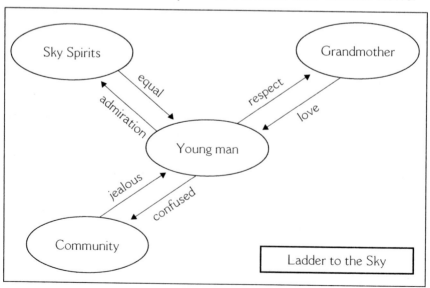

CHARACTER LADDERS

In this activity the names of all the characters are written on card strips, and as a class or in groups children place the characters in rank order from most liked to least liked. Their discussion and subsequent changes in position must provide a reasoned defence for moving individual characters based on their attitude and actions in the tale. Other criteria such as most/least important characters, most/least interesting, most/least complex can also be employed.

EMOTIONS GRAPHS FOR CHARACTER

Creating emotions graphs for particular characters is a way of investigating a character's changing feelings as the story progresses. These can be created for well-known folk-tale characters to perceive the emotional extremes which they experience. For example, contrasting Snow White's emotions with her stepmother's polarised emotional states provides intriguing material for discussion. This can also be related to the depiction of heroes and heroines, good characters and bad ones.

The example from *The Children of Wax* on page 88 shows how the horizontal axis reflects the time span of the tale and the vertical axis reflects the emotional state of the chosen character. Initially significant moments in the tale are listed and mapped on to the graph in an appropriate order, indicating the character's emotional state at each of these points. A phrase to indicate the moment in the tale and an adjective to describe the feelings of the character are added to each marker on the graph. In this example, two nine-year-olds decided to explore the tale from the elder sister's viewpoint. They named her Dineo and through investigating her changing feelings developed a greater understanding of and empathy with her character.

Building on the insight gained through the emotions graph, children can be offered the opportunity to retell the tale in spoken or written form from their chosen character's point of view. This changes the identity of the storyteller and prompts retelling from an insider's perspective.

A graph to show Dineo's feelings in The Children of Wax

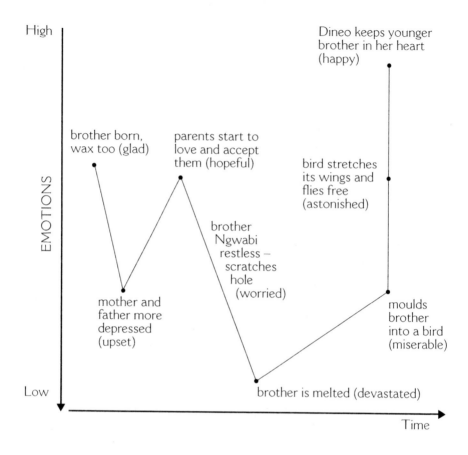

RETELLING FROM A CHARACTER'S PERSPECTIVE

From the same story, Catherine, aged nine, produced this written retelling after she had worked on an emotions graph which examined young Ngwabi's perspective. The position she adopted was that of the 'hero' and therefore she told the tale from his point of view, not in the voice of the narrator.

As a boy I was different from other children, for my brothers, sisters and I were made entirely of wax. My parents called me Ngwabi. I used to wish and wish and wish I had flesh and bones, and they do say 'wishes can come true'. I had a gloomy life for we had to play in our dark hut during the day and at night we would go into the fields and work. When the sun began to rise over the towering mountains we would race back to the hut because the sun would harm us. But at night you could not see birds flying or children laughing and playing. I was a very downcast child.

I scraped a tiny crack in the wall of our hut so I could watch real children at play, and listen to real laughter. I used to dream of being ordinary. In my dreams I climbed the mountains and played with other children. In my dreams I was happy.

One day I could bear it no longer. I ran out of the door into the real world, the daylight. I was ecstatic. I loved the feeling of freedom, the energy, the hot sun on my back, my melting back. I was melting! I yelled to my brothers and sisters, but of course they could not help for they had seen what would happen to them. I screamed uncontrollably.

That night my brothers and sisters came to look at me. I was just a pool of wax lying at their feet, nearly dead and dry. My eldest sister picked me up and gently moulded me, shaped me and formed me into a bird! Leaves were stuck on my wings. I was taken in a ceremonial service to my parents who both kissed me – a goodbye kiss. Then I was lovingly placed on our special stone where we often sat and talked. Finally, my brothers and sisters ran away from me back to the hut.

The next day, as the sun warmed my back again, I felt my feathery wings spreading out. I could fly. I flew high in the sky – oh, the feeling of freedom and energy was wonderful. Maybe wishes do come true. I realised I would have to make my own life, and leave the people I cared for. I circled the hut three times, another kind of goodbye. Six tearful eyes peered back at me through the crack in our hut. I stiffened and looked forwards. The next thing I knew I was soaring high above the mountains. A tune began to float from my mouth. I was finally free!

The discussion and debate that had followed the original storytelling which had been extended through the emotions graph, and the week in-between the graph and the written retelling, provided Catherine with the time and opportunity to inhabit Ngwabi's perspective and to 'dwell inside' the tale. This enabled her to let her thoughts unfold in words on paper, and highlights the need to give children time for development and the opportunity to revisit 'old' tales which may lie untouched in the unconscious until they are ready to be retold.

There are several books which take well-known tales and retell them from a participant's perspective rather than in the more distant voice of the narrator. These offer significant support for developing awareness of characters' alternative perspectives. Particularly recommended are David Henry Wilson's 'Twelve tall and terrible tales' in *There's a Wolf in my Pudding*, Jan Scieszka and Lane Smith's *The True Story of the Three Little Pigs*, retold from the wolf's viewpoint, and Gwen Strauss's collection of poetry entitled *The Trail of Stones* in which the views of various well-known folk-tale characters are described in perceptive and emotive verse (see Appendix 1, pages 165–79).

REFLECTING ON STORYTELLING

It is worth spending time in the classroom reflecting upon the history and purpose of storytelling and on the characteristic features of traditional tales. This will be particularly useful within the context of a storytelling project or unit of work on story. It can develop children's knowledge about language, and help them synthesise what has been learned about the nature of this art form.

> If you cannot increase reflective power in people, you might as well not teach, because reflection is the only thing in the long run that teaches anybody... reflection is what makes the knowing something that can be touched on and assimilated for later use.
>
> Heathcote (1976)

Children's implicit knowledge about language div‹ accent, dialect, register and speech styles as well as the r paralinguistic features in storytelling can all be made more explicit if opportunities in conferences and informal discussions about taped drafts and so on are capitalised upon. Many of the activities discussed in earlier sections will raise awareness of the nature of telling stories. There are, however, additional strategies which explicitly focus on story language and the experience of being a storyteller.

REFLECTING UPON THE LANGUAGE OF STORYTELLING

Reflection upon the language of storytelling can be encouraged in various ways. The figurative language in traditional tales is often rich and worth attention. Extracts from the text can be recorded on card and discussed, categorised or ordered by groups. Repetitive refrains or chants can be made into posters to encourage joining in or to aid later written adaptations. Reading written retellings, children can share their favourite sections or sentences, and explain their choices with reference to the text. Through giving children the chance both to reflect upon the language options taken up by storytellers and to examine the imaginative use of language in traditional tales, their linguistic repertoire can be widened and their productive capacity enhanced, Taylor (1994).

Children often reproduce language patterns from tales which resurface in structurally similar forms in their own stories. For example, during a story circle in which the class were retelling *The Sea Tiger* from Terry Jones's excellent collection *Fairy Tales*, the phrase 'Well, if there's one thing a tiger can't stand it's heights and if there's another thing a tiger can't stand it's water and if there's another thing a tiger...' had been repeatedly used. This phrase is revisited in the tale to accompany each of the tiger's adventures. The class had observed and discussed this linguistic feature prior to their story-circle retelling where it was repeatedly used.

Several weeks later, Nashwin, aged nine, drafted his chosen retelling of an Irish tale about a miser on to tape. This extract from his story used the same linguistic phrase as *The Sea Tiger*.

> Well, if there's one thing a miser can't stand it's banks, and if there's another thing a miser can't stand it's building societies. He wanted to keep it all, all to himself, to count and to touch.

Nashwin repeated this phrase each time the miser counted his gold, and made it clear that he was conscious of using this language feature.

The differences between oral and written retellings are also worth reflecting upon, to highlight how creative voice play and paralinguistic features act as additional layers of meaning. There is no absolute distinction, however, between oral and literate traditions as many story writers borrow features from the oral tradition and vice versa. Considering the effects of their alternative story versions will also prompt reflection upon language as children seek to articulate how parts of the tale changed in their written or oral retelling. Comparing and contrasting published retellings of *Snow White* or *Cinderella*, for example, can also highlight the differences in tone and style of telling which authors and illustrators have adopted.

REFLECTING UPON THE EXPERIENCE OF TELLING TALES

Reflection upon the experience of telling tales can prompt children to consider the process and evaluate the pleasures and challenges involved in this art form. As noted earlier, children can redraft their tales and reflect upon the content and style of their oral stories.

Children's spoken comments on their experience as storytellers suggest that the process of telling contributes to their confidence and helps to make use of the skills that have been developed.

'When we told our stories to Class 3 it was different from telling a story to a friend. I was worried in case they didn't like the story, but I did loads of actions and they had an expression on their faces that said they were listening and that made me feel good.'

'I was nervous at first, but when they listened and laughed it was great. I even added some new bits and used my voice a lot more. I could never have done that last week.'

Written reflections on the experience of storytelling are also valuable. These examples extracted from written learning logs indicate how a dialogue on paper with the teacher and oneself can provoke reflection. Collette, aged seven, was writing after a storytelling afternoon which was the culmination of half a term's work. Sheena, aged nine, noted her comments after listening to her story draft on tape.

It began well but it sounds boring after a while, sort of flat. I must make my voice interesting. I missed out the part about the creatures being stilled at midnight and did more about Bernez being in love. Next time I'll add some noises to the forest and really scream when he falls. It needs to sound more frightening.

Sheena

When I just started telling stories I thought it was scary. It was hard to put expressions in our voices. I told my mum lots of stories. Today I did a story called The Wolf's tail. I made it different to Mrs Grainger's story. It went great.

Collette

Children can set targets for themselves by considering the challenging aspects of storytelling. Questionnaires can also prompt reflection and enhance the status of tale telling. These may be particularly useful within a storytelling project. The discussions can be recorded and displayed as flow diagrams or webs, or if written responses are given these can be used to

supplement a wall display of photographs of the children as storytellers. Possible starter questions might include:
- ❖ Who tells us stories?
- ❖ Where do stories come from?
- ❖ Who do you tell stories to?
- ❖ Do you prefer stories being read to you or told to you?
- ❖ What are traditional tales?
- ❖ Do you like telling stories and if so why?
- ❖ Is there anything hard about storytelling?

Children's responses can be revealing and enable them to articulate their knowledge and understanding about storytelling. At the close of a project, it is particularly interesting to reflect on why the children think they have been telling stories. Some seven-year-olds' responses included:

> 'To put cheerfulness and hope in people.'
> 'To find out what others think of your story and get them to listen.'
> 'So that we get good ideas for our writing.'
> 'To find out how other people think and what people do.'
> 'So we can go into a place of our own and really use our imagination and our own words.'

Another strategy which can prompt consideration and reflection upon this art form is for the class to produce a beginner's guide to storytelling. This could include a rationale, a historical perspective, tips for remembering tales, possible performance skills to develop, and even one or two traditional tales or an accompanying taped collection. This guide could be prepared for another class or could be added to the school's 'Traditional tales resource box'.

Talking and writing about storytelling in these ways can give children additional insights into the artistry and innovation involved in traditional storytelling, and can help them develop the confidence and conscious awareness to evaluate their talk, considering both what they say and how they communicate it.

THE FINAL VICTORY
An Inuit tale

In the days even before our grandfathers were born, many thin and watery moons ago, there lived two great Inuit hunters, Tuk and Nahnuk. These mighty hunters were rightly proud of their skills, for they could easily capture seals on the ice floes, stealthily slay bears in the hunting ground and cleverly harpoon fish in the deep waters and the rapids.

But while these two men were successful hunters and valued within the community, they were also great rivals. For if Tuk were to return with the pelt of a great white bear, then Nahnuk would not rest until he also had slain one. Or if Nahnuk caught a seal, then Tuk would seek a larger one. They were indeed great rivals, always boasting about their most recent catch, trying to prove that each was the better hunter. There were many people who feared for the lives of Tuk and Nahnuk, for these two would think nothing of risking everything in their vain attempts to prove themselves victorious. The villagers were dependent upon the meat and the skins these hunters brought home with them, so they did not know what to do.

As the months passed by and the winter gales were replaced by slightly less chilling winds, the time of the Silver Fish arrived. Tuk and Nahnuk both took to the waters, for the Silver Fish was much prized for its full flavour and the gleaming silver scales that skirted in a pattern along its sides.

Now the winter ice floes had reduced the hunting grounds somewhat that year and it was not long before the kayaks of Tuk and Nahnuk came close together. They shouted to one another, their proud words biting across the icy waters proclaiming their prowess. The wind grew wilder and in response to its fits and squalls the two hunters needed all their skill to keep their kayaks afloat. When the wind finally abated they found their known landmarks were gone. They did not recognise the ice peaks around them and, utterly exhausted, were forced to land upon a nearby island. Scraping their boats up on the hardened ice, neither man spoke to the other, but eyed each other bitterly with a deep sense of loathing, for each of the rivals secretly blamed the other for his misfortune. A strange sound broke the tense silence, a sound neither had ever heard before...

A high-pitched giggle and small squeals of laughter rang out across the icy crevices, and Nahnuk crept cautiously over a large bank of snow. He saw before him three tiny dwarfs, rocking backwards and forwards with glee as they joked, laughed and poked each other's tiny bellies. Nahnuk's eyes lit up and he lunged forward and grabbed the smallest dwarf. The other two sprang downwards and disappeared into holes in the snow. The captured dwarf was frantic, screaming and struggling, but Nahnuk held on determinedly. He knew that this prize would prove him the greater hunter once and for all.

Triumphantly he returned to Tuk, brandishing his prize and refusing to listen to his rival who spoke with concern of the wind gods' revenge. 'You must know, my brother, that the wind gods protect these tiny creatures.

They will surely seek retribution if you imprison him!' But Nahnuk did not trust Tuk, nor did he heed his warning. He took his harpoon and, fastening a leather thong to the end, plunged it deep into the ice. Then he tied the dwarf to the remaining leather and tethered him to the harpoon like a wild animal.

By now, night was falling and it was too late for the rivals to return home, so they were forced to make shelters for the night out of the skins and spears in their kayaks. All the while the dwarf wriggled, pinned down as he was in the snow, and called out in desperation to the wind gods to save him, to rescue him. Nahnuk lost patience with his high-pitched squeals and struck out at the dwarf, hitting him ruthlessly across the face and swearing at him to hold his tongue. Tuk crawled silently into his makeshift shelter, but the wind growled and grumbled, stalking around their tents like some terrible animal. Neither hunter could sleep. The noise of the wind roaring, whirling and howling outside seared through their very bones.

Strangely, Tuk thought he heard a voice calling to him on the wind. He strained to listen and could hardly distinguish the words which seemed to whisper, 'Pour water on your tent, pour water on your tent, pour water on your tent.'

Afraid of the wrath of the wind gods, yet unsure of his task, Tuk struggled out of his shelter and ventured to his kayak at the water's edge. Inside the kayak he found two sealskin pouches and, dipping these deep into the dark and freezing waters, he filled them with water and returned to his shelter, spattering icy water all over it. The words on the wind persisted, however, and whispered in his ear, 'Pour water on your tent, pour water on your tent, pour water on your tent.'

So once again, and many times that dark night, Tuk went down to the black sea, scooped up water and stumbled back in the bitter cold to pour water on his tent. Again and again, his furs were almost blown from him, his fingers became numb with the cold, and his eyes watered and stung. Finally, it seemed to him that he could hear the voices no more and, returning to his tent in sheer exhaustion, he fell into a deep sleep.

The next morning when Tuk awoke, he found around him a great whiteness, a bright hard shell of ice: the very first igloo. Taking his pick he hacked his way out of the ice house and stepped on to the snow outside. There before him lay Nahnuk's lifeless body. His shelter had been blown away by the wind, and he had frozen to death. The harpoon was still deep in the ice, but the thong that had tied the dwarf's body to it was chewed through. The dwarf was gone, and it had even taken Nahnuk's Inuit spirit with him.

CHAPTER 4

EXPLORING TRADITIONAL TALES THROUGH ROLE-PLAY AND DRAMA

Role-play and drama can significantly enrich the story-making and storytelling culture of the classroom. The narrative provides the learner with a powerful hook to prompt exploration and gives form to the drama which in turn offers the techniques to undertake the story journey. In classroom storydrama children become the co-authors of the tale as it is created, investigated and shaped by them. Dramatic exploration in this form, whether with puppets, in a role-play area, or with the class as a whole, is not a process of re-enactment, when a known tale is performed, but a process of collective enquiry; a living through literature which demands an active and imaginative involvement inside the layers of the tale. By walking in role in different characters' shoes, children enter vicariously into the world of others, live their lives, learn from their stories and gain insight into their own.

The pioneering work of Dorothy Heathcote (1976) and Gavin Bolton (1984) underpins this drama for understanding, which works towards 'innerstanding', as Heathcote describes it. This chapter explores imaginative play contexts which support storytelling and oral story making, for imagining is enriched by tales told, tales read and tales investigated in drama.

> The worlds of children's play are like the worlds we recognize in novels. Both are created by the power of our fictive imagining.
>
> Meek (1990)

CO-CREATING TALES THROUGH STORYDRAMA

Classroom storydrama offers the opportunity for children to stretch their understanding of traditional tales, to question them actively and through their engagement to restructure or re-vision such tales from the inside. Simultaneously, storydrama prompts storytelling, both informal and personal telling, as well as telling in a more literary style. In storydrama children and teachers alike, individually and collectively, are potential storytellers, story listeners and story makers. If children simply re-enact an oral story and perform it, they are led by the known plot line and will not be encouraged to hypothesise, question or reshape the meanings in the tale. Storydrama is not developed through stories retold in action. It is a process of discovery, which allows the children to linger within the tale, to examine its issues and dig beneath the surface of the words in order to create new meanings, new understandings and to make learning happen.

> The story and its strength enable the teacher to dip into the richness of the contexts that the author has provided. Drama becomes a tool for the exploration of the ideas, relationships and language of the story.
>
> Booth (1987)

Teachers can use any fiction for this work, but the literary prose of books is not as flexible as spoken story words which can be shaped and reshaped in the mouth of the teller. In using oral stories from traditional folklore, the teacher is providing rich material for investigation, since folk tales are at the basis of much human knowledge and understanding and examine archetypal concerns about the human condition. Further, in relying on the power of traditional tales, and by telling tales, not reading them, the teacher is free to act as a creative narrator as the story unfolds. So the children's contributions and ideas are honoured and included in the ongoing telling. Another advantage in telling traditional tales in this context is that the social and communal nature of this art form enables children to step easily into the 'now time' of the tale. There are no book barriers or illustrators' orientations to contend with; just the power of the spoken word and tale to tempt the children into a make-believe world in which they are the corporate creators.

This section examines ways of using traditional folklore in drama. Three strategies are detailed: exploring the language of the unsaid in a tale, building from a story fragment, and taking the tale as the guide. The last tends to be more teacher-directed and less open-ended than the others, but much will depend upon the teacher's professional judgement and the nature of the learning focus. Common to all three strategies, however, is the range of drama techniques that the teacher can use to structure the drama work and help the children learn through discovery and imagined experience. (A glossary of these techniques and conventions is on pages 183–6.) The section concludes with possible extension activities which can arise from such classroom storydrama. The comfortable context of the classroom is preferable as a site for such investigations, providing the privacy, resources and time which a hall session cannot offer.

EXPLORING THE LANGUAGE
OF THE UNSAID IN A TALE

An easy access route into storydrama is to examine retrospectively the unspoken language of the tale. Inevitably there will be gaps or omissions in the tale: moments of tension or indecision which are left undeveloped; characters whose conversation and offstage behaviour remain unrecorded; leaps in the narrative which cross years of unchartered territory. As Iser (1979) argues, 'No tale can be told in its entirety', and the children's hypotheses about the characters, the action and the issues can be explored by filling in the gaps left by the text. These unspoken elements can be investigated in drama to deepen the children's understanding and illuminate the meanings within the story.

Following a retelling of *The Weaving of a Dream* (see pages 161–4), for example, the class can be asked to identify the parts of the story which interested or puzzled them. Some of the questions posed by children have included:

'Why was the woman so obsessed with the painting?'
'What happened to the father?'
'Is the whole story just a dream?'
'What did the two brothers do in the city?'
'Who was the old crone?'

Gradually, the children become more adept at asking questions which are ripe for dramatic exploration as they seek to unravel undeveloped elements of the tale. This technique, developed from Aidan Chambers' (1993) work, is useful to open dramatic contexts, since the questions and puzzles the children themselves identify are often much more pertinent than the ones teachers ask. The knowledge that the question may be investigated in drama serves to heighten the children's interest and to prompt much reflective discussion. Following small-group discussion of the various suggestions, the class can vote on which questions to illuminate through drama. This ensures that the children themselves direct their own enquiries. Using a range of drama techniques, such as role-play, improvisation, freeze-frames and so on, the teacher and the class are released from the storyline to investigate the tale.

One class of ten- to eleven-year-olds were very curious about the old crone in *The Weaving of a Dream*. In small groups the children re-created and improvised scenes from the woman's childhood, developing 'inference in action', based on the tale. Later, in role as her parents, they shared their hopes, expectations and concerns for their daughter. Freeze-frames were created depicting a previous incident in which she showed her mystical power, and her thoughts and feelings were heard when she chose to live alone in her stone abode. Finally, the old crone was hot seated, while the rest of the class, in role as journalists from the big city, quizzed her about her unearthly knowledge of the past, present and future. The newspaper articles some children later chose to write variously declaimed her as 'nothing but a witch' and 'a senile old woman who lives in a world of dreams'. Others celebrated her foresight as 'a wise woman indeed' and 'a natural godmother to us all'. Similar characters in other tales were also identified.

The drama techniques used in this example served to create a life history for the woman, a partial biography experienced in action. Her story was later retold on to tape autobiographically, in which 'she' explained that the powers of nature had always directed her through her dreams. Now that she had helped return the woven dream, she could dream no more. Her psychic energy was spent; she was lost and alone.

Through inhabiting the language of the unsaid in this and other tales, children create new stories. Such fictive insights are very satisfying and enable learners to know and understand that much more has been shared in a tale than appears in its surface features or syntax. Storydrama provides the opportunity for storytelling as well as collective story investigation and creation.

A variation on this strategy is to perceive the tale as only the first chapter and, through storydrama, invent further chapters. A new, unspoken narrative will unfold as the children improvise their follow-up tale.

For example, in a class of five- to six-year-olds a letter was received from a fictional member of the class who had lost his St Christopher medallion in the Giant's castle at the top of the beanstalk. The class had performed *Jack and the Beanstalk* for assembly, and were eager to extend the tale. They borrowed ladders from a builders' yard and ascended to new heights in their adventures in the clouds, hunting for the medallion. New tales emerged from the old one and the class met various characters, including the Giant's widow, who retold the encounter with Jack from her point of view. Within the broad frame of each traditional tale lie untold tales waiting to be uncovered and explored.

BUILDING FROM A STORY FRAGMENT:
THE OPENING SCENARIO

An alternative strategy combining traditional tales and storydrama is to select a single scenario from an unknown tale, as a beginning for dramatic exploration. If only the opening elements of a tale are told, then children can construct their own story. The narrative will unfold at the very moment of engagement in the drama. However, if this entry into drama is employed it is important to avoid the 'what happened next' syndrome, which drives the drama into developing a plot line at the expense of digging down into the internal dynamics of the situation.

The first part of *The End of Baba Yaga* (see pages 31–2) makes an effective launch pad. The maiden Vasseila, living with her father and two cruel stepsisters, is obliged to venture out into the dark to visit Baba Yaga, a carnivorous witch woman. As she enters the wood, the wind whips about her cloak and strange noises emanate from the darkness. To leave the storytelling having set the scene, signalled the genre, introduced some characters and presented a problem furnishes the children with the foundations of their drama. The story provides a potential dramatic context and the drama itself structures *their* story, not in a series of sequential events but through the use of flashbacks, flash forwards (the depiction of scenes occurring in the future), improvisations and other techniques. In this case the scene Vasseila left behind at home could be improvised, or freeze-frames of an 'encounter' or difficulty in the woods could be depicted.

Learning to work co-operatively, children will incorporate the additional information created by their colleagues into their unfolding story. Predicting an event which occurred three days later and improvising that could also prompt engagement with the tale. In role, characters could recall the local folk tales known about Baba Yaga or the myths about the Great White Knight. Such tellings may be developed tales or brief anecdotes, but all such stories can be discovered within the ongoing drama, and engage the children's imagination and interest. Following the creation of the class's version of Vasseila's encounter with Baba Yaga, the story could be retold from different characters' points of view. Such tellings avoid the restrictive demands of getting the story 'right', and highlight alternative viewpoints and perceptions not necessarily verbalised during the drama.

Children project themselves imaginatively into stories through drama and determine what is important about the story for themselves. In building group images of the characters and the action, the children are co-authoring their own tale, establishing and negotiating agreed knowledge, and then sifting and evaluating the issues and consequences for evidence and meaning. The 'original' Baba Yaga story itself could be told at some later date. Certainly, the children will be motivated to read some of her other adventures, and draw conclusions about her based on their reading and experience. Improvisations building on merely the title or theme of a tale are also possible to use as opening story fragments.

BUILDING FROM A STORY FRAGMENT:
THE CLOSING SCENARIO

Another fragment of an unknown tale which can set the context for drama is the ending. To share with the class some elements of the last scene can provide the basis for dramatic exploration. The purpose is not to re-create the tale – the children may not even know the scene described is the end of a tale – but to investigate the past, present and future of the characters/situation described in the light of limited information. In drama, time can be controlled and examined, explored in actions and words. At the conclusion of the drama the teacher can share the source tale, and to this storytelling the class bring their insights and understanding developed from the parallel themes and related issues which they placed upon the agenda of *their* storydrama.

For example, an Irish folk tale about Tir-Nan-Oge, which is 'The Land of the Ever Young', ends with the young warrior, Usheen, riding proudly into a small village square. He looks around searchingly, then his eyes alight upon an old stone water trough, which he rides over to. Smiling with satisfaction, he dismounts from his steed. Immediately his body begins to shrivel, wrinkles pinch his face, and Usheen appears to age rapidly. Seconds later he dies.

To share this extract with a class and couple it with the statement 'Those who take more than their fair share receive their just rewards' provides an interesting fragment to explore. The class can improvise episodes in Usheen's life, create his last conversation and freeze-frame the images that passed through his mind as he died. Groups can then test out their ideas on one another and create a collective sense of the character of Usheen as they search for a connection between his life history and the story statement. An excellent retelling of this tale can be found in Betty Rosen's (1993) book *Shapers and Polishers*.

Storydrama is a way of remaking the past, exploring the future and understanding the present, and in choosing fragments of tales the teacher is drawing upon the rich resources of folklore. *The Children of Wax* (see pages 56–7) lends itself to extracting story fragments and combining these with ambiguous story statements as does *Ladder to the Sky* (see pages 11–12). Through using drama techniques, the children build with their teacher a storydrama which motivates and challenges them. They will be involved in creating many new texts and tales as they do so, and shaping their own learning in the process.

TAKING THE TALE AS THE GUIDE

A strategy which leans more overtly on the tale to prompt improvisation and investigation is that of taking the tale as the guide. The teacher tells the tale, stopping intermittently to ask the children how they could, through drama, find out more about the characters, the mood, conflict or issues in the story. After some dramatic exploration the tale is taken up again by the teacher who incorporates the new collective elements in her storytelling and shares more of the tale. In this way the story provokes the drama, which in turn provides a context for further story making and storytelling.

A supportive feature of this strategy is that for the inexperienced drama practitioner the tale acts as a mentor or guide. As in many classroom contexts, however, the teacher is left to exercise her judgement about when to stay close to the story structure, exploring themes along the way, and when to leave the tale behind and focus on the class's interests and concerns. In this sense this third strategy enables the class to explore the language of the unsaid and to build from story fragments as they journey alongside the tale. A detailed example of a drama developed from *The Final Victory* (see pages 95–6) in which the tale guided the session is provided on pages 108–16.

Ladder to the Sky (see pages 11–12) also lends itself to this strategy, with the teacher as a storyteller using the beginning of the story to set a common context, a sense of place. Halting the tale, the children could be asked to role-play parent–child conversations about the vine, or later to create the local gossip and stories shared about the young man who seemed to be favoured by the spirits. His stoning could also be depicted in tableaux. In one class of nine- to ten-year-olds I stopped the drama after such tableaux and asked the children, 'What do you think the village would do in this situation? How could they solve this problem?' A disciplinary meeting was decided upon in which 'Surefoot' (as the children named the young man) would be interviewed. I volunteered to take his role and was told by the Shaman to 'wait outside until we call you'. Much debate ensued and villagers told tales of my exploits, what they had seen, suspected and believed. When I entered I was told to sit in the centre of their circle and asked to swear to the Great Manitou to tell the truth. I answered many questions, mostly ambiguously in order to challenge their thinking, admitted little and suggested that the Great Manitou himself was to blame.

After the meeting the children chose a form of writing to share their thinking. Their work included diaries, poetry, letters and news reports. Simon, aged nine years, wrote the following article on page 106.

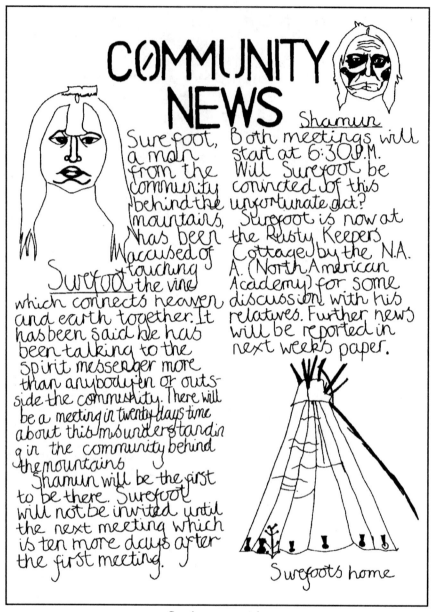

COMMUNITY NEWS

Shamun

Surefoot, a man from the community behind the mountains, has been accused of touching the vine which connects heaven and earth together. It has been said he has been talking to the spirit messenger more than anybody in or outside the community. There will be a meeting in twenty days time about this misunderstanding in the community behind the mountains. Shamun will be the first to be there. Surefoot will not be invited until the next meeting which is ten more days after the first meeting.

Both meetings will start at 6:30 P.M. Will Surefoot be convicted of this unfortunate act? Surefoot is now at the Rusty Keepers Cottage by the N.A.A. (North American Academy) for some discussion with his relatives. Further news will be reported in next week's paper.

Surefoots home

Sam's news article

His words demonstrate his engagement and understanding. After their writing, the tale continued to guide the drama, enabling the children to develop areas of interest, give form and shape to their ideas, and be storytellers themselves.

EXTENDING THE STORYDRAMA

Following an exploration of a tale through drama, whether the class has explored the language of the unsaid, built a new story from a small fragment or taken the tale as their guide, there will be opportunities to extend this work in a variety of ways. Activities across the whole breadth of the curriculum can be undertaken in the arts, humanities and the sciences. However, if the class is to retain the sense of 'digging down' into the story itself, then creating tenuous curriculum links should be assiduously avoided. The story may well have been selected to complement a topic theme, but the issues raised in the storydrama will be the children's own. It is important, therefore, that some choice be given to the children and that, together, the teacher and the class generate possible ideas for follow-up work. Such work has the potential to extend the storydrama, give voice to the response generated and build upon the insights gained.

Retelling the tale from particular viewpoints, or reliving sections of the tale through taped role-play, can develop new angles and perspectives. Playscripts of scenes could emerge from this work, or oral drafts of later presentations about issues in the tale. Using *The Weaving of a Dream* (see pages 161–4), for example, groups might draft their arguments about the central theme in the tale. Children's suggestions have included 'Life is a journey', 'Dreams can come true' and 'A test of love'. Taping their draft presentations enables the children to refine and polish their work before presenting it to the class.

Writing in role is also a valuable extension technique. Whose diary entry would the children choose to write and from what point in the tale? What newspaper accounts or historical records can be composed which detail the events? Could the tale be painted, storyboarded, used as a stimulus for dance or as an inspiration for poetry? Given the choice, the children often find a medium and a form which supports or extends their textual encounter. It is worth stressing, however, that although storydrama can tap language competencies which might otherwise remain hidden, the insistence that all storydrama work is followed up can deaden its potential. Do the children themselves need to be the final arbiters here? Do they wish to extend this work? Now? Later? Not at all? Does the teacher want them to capitalise upon their engagement immediately, or leave a period of mulling over, an 'incubatory period', as James Britton (1982) calls it, prior to revisiting the issues? Perhaps a reflective discussion about the tale will suffice. The choice of follow-up is a sensitive one and will vary according to context and purpose.

Drama and storytelling work together to enhance children's potential and literacy learning: by encouraging reading, enabling writing, and prompting talking and listening. Children experience some of the rich alternatives and possibilities open to storytellers and writers as they actively examine the spirit of the story and co-author new tales through drama. This is an endless empowering and self-replenishing source for learning.

EXPLORING 'THE FINAL VICTORY' THROUGH CLASSROOM DRAMA

This storydrama evolved through using the technique of 'taking the tale as our guide'. I told the class the tale of *The Final Victory* (see pages 95–6), stopped intermittently and used drama conventions to investigate aspects of the tale. At the close of the tale I encouraged the children to take the story one stage further in drama and then worked with them on a range of follow-up activities. The class comprised thirty-four eight- to eleven-year-olds in a tiny village school in rural Kent. The first part of the drama session, which ended with tableaux to embody the meaning of the tale, took approximately an hour and a quarter. The extension activities which were planned following the drama were undertaken after break and before lunch. Later, several children chose to redraft, edit and extend their work. The intention was not to re-enact the tale, nor to merely role-play undeveloped aspects but to use dramatic forms and techniques to explore the themes within the story and to work towards an understanding of these issues.

THE DRAMA DEVELOPS AS THE STORY UNFOLDS

As a teacher I chose this story to examine the issue of rivalry: the ways in which rivals react and behave towards one another and the consequences of such a fiercely competitive ethos for all involved. I began by boasting of how that very morning I'd managed to park my car in a minimal space between two others, and then invited the class to think of something that they were good at and could boast about. In pairs for a few minutes we boasted of our skills, and then discussed in fours what kinds of things people boast about and why. These anecdotes provided a personal introduction to the theme of the story which I then began to tell, sharing the first section of the tale about the competitive ways of Tuk and Nahnuk.

Having set the scene through storytelling, I invited the children, in pairs, to take up roles as Tuk and Nahnuk and to prove verbally that they were the greater hunter. Some of the pairs then shared snippets of these conversations, and we learned that Tuk had proved his strength earlier when wrestling with a bear, that Nahnuk descended from a long line of hunters, that Tuk could catch more fish from the icy waters, and other details.

I told more of the story and included their boasts and arguments, explaining that the villagers who were dependent on these two hunters were worried that the two men were risking their lives in trying to prove their prowess. I stopped the storytelling again to help the children start to create a collective image of the community as a whole. Taking up a role as an elder of the tribe, I suggested we held a meeting to seek a solution to our problem. The class took up this proposal readily and seated themselves naturally in a circle.

A litany of complaints and concerns poured from the group. One member told the village how he had recently seen Tuk risk his life on the ice floes. Others noted that in going further afield to hunt for bigger prey the regular provision was being reduced. Many moaned about the relentless arguing. 'My children cannot sleep at night while they shout and boast,' one parent complained, 'something must be done.'

'They have been like this since birth,' Tuk's mother informed the class, 'always boasting and fighting.'

Gradually a series of proposals emerged. Should we ask them to train some younger men, or would this lead to two rival groups, even armies, in our community? Should we set them a challenge to the death and accept only one hunter? Tuk's mother squashed that suggestion vehemently, but in any case it was realised that supplies would suffer. Should we meet them as a group and explain our concerns? Should they be disciplined? Should we pray for them?

At a lull in the proceedings I took up the story again, explaining that even as the villagers sat late into the night debating, Tuk and Nahnuk were at that moment packing their kayaks ready for an early start the following day. For it was the season of the Silver Fish and each was keen to be the first to return with this valued prize. I told of how the storm blew up and how both were stranded on a strange island, silently blaming each other for their misfortune. 'A strange sound broke the silence, a sound neither had ever heard before...'

Turning to the class, I asked the children to work in small groups to create tableaux showing the source of the noise. These variously depicted the Silver Fish flapping and stranded on the ice, a bear groaning, an ice dragon in his lair, and a tribe of fierce Inuit hunters sharpening their spears. At this point I could have asked the class to vote on which scenario they wanted to investigate and used the story so far as a stepping-stone. However, I made the choice to remain guided by the tale, still stopping intermittently to give the class ownership of the dramatic context and the chance to investigate the text of the tale as it unfolded. They heard how Nahnuk captured the dwarf and pinned it down in the snow, of Tuk warning his rival of the wrath of the wind gods, and the dwarf plaintively praying for protection. In a momentary pause at this point, Matthew suggested, 'We could do the dwarf's cries, Miss.' The class discussed possible phrases and requests and we all knelt in the snow together in role as the dwarf and made our pleas to the wind. These monologues filled the classroom with echoes of despair, and I was easily able to rejoin the story over the last pitiful cries by exposing Nahnuk's cruelty to the dwarf; his unjust response to his prisoner's prayers.

Reaching the completion of the tale, when Tuk hacks his way out of the igloo to find the dead body of his rival in the snow, I extended the story, and narrated Tuk's return to the community, telling the class that he towed back Nahnuk's kayak in which his body had been placed. In role as Tuk, I looked slowly around and muttered, 'It wasn't my fault!' and awaited their response. Having been guided by the tale thus far, and having to some extent controlled (though not directed) the drama through the storytelling, I was now offering them the open chance to explore the villagers' response to this situation. I hoped the shift in register from the more formal voice of the storyteller to my informal words as Tuk had signalled this.

There were seconds of silence. Some children began to view me with obvious contempt; a few gathered around a space symbolising the kayak with Nahnuk's body in it, shaking their heads and giving me solemn glances. No one came forward to greet me, yet all had heard the tale. I wasn't to blame, surely? 'It wasn't my fault,' I repeated.

'That is for us to decide,' snapped one boy.

'What evidence have you?' asked another.

I was then treated to a barrage of relatively aggressive questions, during which I tried to explain the truth as I saw it. A couple of people acknowledged that they had heard stories of the wind gods, although many denounced such tales as 'just stories', 'lies' and 'nonsense'. Some refused to believe my description of the ice house, so I promised to try to build one for the village. This did appease a few, but most continued to mistrust my tale, demanding proof that I had not killed Nahnuk.

'You have blood on your hands. How do you explain that?' one villager demanded to know. In role I was encouraging the children to question me, to 'hot seat' the character Tuk in their search for knowledge and understanding.

An elder emerged who claimed that as chief it was his job to hear all the views and decide my fate. I appealed to my mother for support, looking openly about me. A girl stepped forward, looked at me directly and asked calmly, 'How can you hold your head up here? Even his spirit is gone. I am ashamed of you.'

Before I could reply, she had turned away. Gradually, however, some supportive voices emerged, requesting a decent burial for the deceased, and a fair trial for Tuk. One villager even voiced the view that Nahnuk had got what he deserved. To close this improvisation I declared my rights, reiterated my position and told them truthfully that I was grieved it had turned out this way.

We then drew around one child's body to represent the deceased Nahnuk, and in a ritual fashion gathered at the hunter's grave, recording our thoughts within the outline of the body. Some of the inscriptions written in role included:

> 'I am sorry this had to happen.'
> 'We should have done more to solve the problem.'
> 'A violent beginning and a violent end.'
> 'You broke the laws of the gods, but did you deserve this?'
> 'It is not my fault, yet I feel partly to blame.'

The sensitivity of many of their responses which we read together demonstrated that the children were beginning to grasp the complexity of the situation, and some were developing a sense of human empathy and community responsibility.

Finally, I asked the class to create tableaux which summed up what *The Final Victory* was really about, a symbolic representation of the story's meaning with an accompanying caption. The groups' discussions and debates were intense. Their final tableaux included Tuk standing sorrowfully beside Nahnuk's body entitled 'Victory?'; a large human-made mouth entitled 'Jealousy eats you up'; a bevy of fists entitled 'Fighting to be first'; and a group of villagers and Tuk at Nahnuk's grave looking at each other, entitled 'Who's to blame?' One group simply looked at each other suspiciously and named their tableau 'Broken trust'. The last group, their backs to each other, looked impassively over their shoulders into the space between them, captioning their image 'Neither black nor white'.

Working together with the story as their guide, the children had incorporated fresh pieces of information from each other into the tale, and told tales from their collective imaginary past as well as some which reflected personal experience. Simultaneously they had explored feelings and jointly constructed meanings, digging beneath the surface of *The Final Victory* to develop a sense of insight and understanding. Their final freeze-frames provided evidence that the theme of competitive rivalry had been illuminated, reflected upon in different ways, explored and evaluated by the learners through this blend of classroom drama and storytelling. I then sought to capitalise upon this session through extension work.

EXTENSION ACTIVITIES DEVELOP
THE STORY FURTHER

I asked the class to make suggestions for follow-up work. They had far more ideas than I had, growing out of their individual engagements with the tale, their previous experience and their knowledge of the web of story possibilities. Together we compiled the following list which I scribed for them, and individually or in pairs or groups they chose an activity to work on from the list.

We could:

✧ retell our tale from another viewpoint;
✧ modernise our tale;
✧ replace our tale in another context;
✧ rewrite part of our tale as a playscript;
✧ write an obituary for Nahnuk;
✧ retell part of our tale on tape;
✧ produce a newspaper report;
✧ write Tuk's diary entry on his return;
✧ design flyers for the film *All for an Igloo*.

The motivating effect of the enactive mode had all the children organising their chosen extension activity very quickly after breaktime. Three chose to work on film flyers; the other thirty-one selected a written or oral option. Having explored and reshaped the meanings in the story, the children now began to represent these threads in other genres. Many found new texts and tales emerged through the interaction of the original tale, the storydrama, their experience, and the style and form of their selected communication. Rapidly, pieces of work rolled off the press, a testament to the power of drama and storytelling.

Replacing the story in China, Richard, aged nine, was frantic. Where could he find a book on the country? He needed the name of an ancient monument which was important enough for two men to fight over. In the end he selected the Great Wall of China and introduced us in his epic to two proud Kung Fu fighters, the mean Fonghi and the tough Le-mo.

Matthew and Gareth, both aged eight, also replaced the tale, this time in the mountains of Cumbria. Their two-headed giants played a deadly game of one-upmanship, razing mountains to the ground.

Jonathan, aged ten, delighted in retelling his modernised tale as a Hollywood spoof. His tale spun on the same axis as *The Final Victory*, developing the theme of rivalry between two film producers. Jonathan had never read *The Final Victory*, nor seen a written version but, through the dramatic storytelling in which he'd engaged, he had clearly imbibed the structure of the tale sufficiently to use it adroitly in his written retelling. His tale involved Stephen Spielberg capturing one of the seven dwarfs to be the star in his next film.

Another modern piece was a playscript entitled 'Mix up'. This acidly depicted Margaret Thatcher and her husband Denis competing over their royal relationships and connections.

Over half of the class chose to stay close to the original story, its setting and characters. Several held on to their final self-selected role as a member of the community and wrote about the events from their point of view. One poignantly adopted the role of Nahnuk's friend and spoke of her conviction that Tuk had murdered Nahnuk, of her sense of loss and of her plans to sway the villagers' views, to seek revenge and to give her friend a decent hunter's burial.

Alex, aged nine, simply wrote the following note-like entries in the chief's diary. This was his idea entirely which he followed up from his earlier role.

Friday 26 November
Tuk and Nahnuk aren't back. Getting a bit worried.
Maybe they've killed each other. What should I do?

Saturday 27 November
Still no sign of them. Their families are very worried. Told them Tuk and Nahnuk bound to come back. Slowly running out of food.

Sunday 28 November
Tuk returned. Alone. Nahnuk's family devastated. Suicide? Murder? He brought no food – no Silver Fish. We must train more hunters. Tomorrow Tuk to talk to a meeting of elders. I don't trust him.

Alex demonstrates the power of role to evoke considerations from different angles and viewpoints. There was no chief mentioned in the original telling, but the story tribe in this class had created a new and communal tale in which a chief elder had taken on the role of judge, an arbiter of the truth. Alex clearly warmed to this role and wished to sustain it through his writing. In suggesting Tuk returned alone, he also changed our story and created more ambiguity and tension.

Dorothy Heathcote (1976) has called such writing 'drama on paper', an apt phrase for these examples which show the children's fictive imagining.

Several of the children, keen to continue the debate and decide Tuk's final fate, argued on tape that he should be publicly demoted as the community hunter since he had been equally to blame. One pair took up the tale from the captured dwarf's viewpoint who was furious with his friends for deserting him in his hour of need. Indeed, in one new story this led to civil war among the dwarf community. Another pair retold the tale in its entirety, taping it with sound effects and adding a narrator's moralistic postscript.

Crispin, aged eight, demonstrated a different response, and identified ecological elements running alongside the story. He wrote a strident letter from a watching seal about the seemingly unnecessary waste of life which Tuk and Nahnuk effected. He demanded to know what the Inuits would do when all the baby seals had been culled, and encouraged them to search for other food. Choosing his position from which to write in role and his form of communication gave Crispin a real audience for writing, a chance to be heard and an opportunity to develop his perspective.

All the extension work demonstrated how a powerful tale explored and investigated through drama and storytelling can become a rich source bank for children to utilise, and a unique springboard for language work that is motivated, varied and has a real sense of personal voice.

STORYTELLING AND STORY MAKING IN ROLE-PLAY AREAS

Imaginative play areas, like storydrama contexts, place children in potentially dramatic situations which are full of opportunities to explore known narratives and develop new ones. In such situations children's role-play provides a vehicle for building on their development as talkers, listeners, readers, writers and tellers of tales. Role-play areas need not be confined to early years classrooms. Indeed, as the HMI (1990) document on *The Teaching and Learning of Drama* highlighted, imaginative play areas provide considerable scope for older children too. In essence, the role-play area is an informal microcosm of classroom storydrama; in it improvisation holds sway as the group creates, investigates and responds to fictional situations. Successful role-play areas are planned along the lines of classroom drama, with the class identifying the people and predicaments which might be encountered in the particular place.

REAL-WORLD AND IMAGINARY ROLE-PLAY AREAS

The majority of role-play areas in classrooms rely upon aspects of functional literacy for their sense of reality, with shops and cafés, hospitals and health centres, schools and offices being popular choices. Such real-world play areas provide sound opportunities for literate play, and appropriate literacy materials are employed to support reading and writing in context. If the teacher is also involved in providing 'real' problems for the cooks, waitresses and customers to solve in the café, then the scope for developing small group drama is capitalised upon. In these areas, anecdotes of personal experience are often retold in role, and this imitative play provides real chances for children to revisit the tales of their own lives, as well as to improvise new situations and scenarios.

However, a balance needs to be achieved between functional real-world areas and role-play areas which are more open-ended, more overtly fictional in their construction. Such contexts are often less well defined, but imaginatively vital in that they allow the children to play, freely building on the foundations of stories. So in the 'Enchanted forest', created in the corner of the classroom, the children are prompted to meet fictional characters from traditional tales, for example, the Big Bad Wolf, Red Riding Hood, a dwarf, a fairy, Baba Yaga or Anancy. Through such encounters the learners are able to engage in their own storydramas with these fictional characters, and play with known tales and the issues and images represented within them.

> If a narrative is being used as the source of a drama, the children can identify with and clarify what is happening in the book, in the drama, and in their own lives.
>
> Booth (1985)

In fiction-based role-play areas, children frequently and deliberately engage in investigating several tales at once, operating together, as Allan Ahlberg does in *Jeremiah in the Dark Woods* at the level of intertextual reference. The stories of their own lives will also weave in and out of their role-play in these areas. Teachers wishing to develop children's storytelling and story-making competence, aligning this with a focus on traditional tales, will want to offer imaginary role-play areas which have some folklore connection.

IMAGINARY ROLE-PLAY AREAS

a castle	the land of nursery rhymes
an enchanted forest	the land at the end of the rainbow
an island	the kingdom under the sea
an underwater cave	the land of the giants
a cottage in the woods	a castle in the clouds
a magic garden	the fairy kingdom
a magician's mansion	the world of the stars

IDENTIFYING POSSIBLE CHARACTERS IN THE IMAGINARY ROLE-PLAY AREA

It is essential to pool children's ideas about the kinds of people, characters and creatures who might be encountered in their role-play area. Their brainstorms and accompanying pictures and posters provide options from which the children can choose for their role-play.

Often, children will add new characters to the class list following their story making, having swapped roles during their play and met other characters in the area. The list of possible characters indicates to the teacher the class's current repertoire of known stories, which together they can draw upon. Children need to know who they are before they can react appropriately in dramatic situations, and in selecting a particular character from a known tale they already have considerable, albeit implicit, knowledge of that character's behaviour, attitude and history. A list made by a class of six- to seven-year-olds for their wood initially included the following:

In our wood we could be:

a witch, a wizard

a wolf, a woodcutter, a huntsman

a princess, tree fairies, elves

teddy bears

Little Red Riding Hood, Grandma

Snow White, the Seven Dwarfs, the Queen

Hansel and Gretel, Rumplestiltskin

Robin Hood, Friar Tuck, Maid Marian

Goldilocks, the Three Bears

Plop, his parents (from *The Owl who was afraid of the Dark* by Jill Tomlinson)

Max, the Wild Things (from *Where the Wild Things Are* by Maurice Sendak)

Baby Owls, their mum (from *Owl Babies* by Martin Waddell)

Denis the Monster, his mum, the boy (from *The Monster Bed* by Jeanne Willis)

The intention is not to direct or limit the role-play or focus it upon re-enactment of traditional tales but to assist children in engaging in imaginative play through initially adopting a particular role. Most groups sort out their roles prior to entering the role-play area and then find that the action and predicaments that they experience require other characters, so there is flexibility. Children who are more used to imitative play in 'real world' print-oriented play areas may at first find the demands of imaginary, more open role-play areas very challenging. This is where traditional tales frequently told and retold by teachers and children, and a developing awareness of scene and a sense of place, offer the learners rich material to build upon. In a classroom where folklore has a high profile, then imaginary role-play areas will be seized upon as places for revisitation, re-examination and investigation of characters, plot and action, as well as contexts for the creation of new tales which grow from the seeds of the old. Through role-play in such areas, children can challenge as well as explore fictional people, develop empathy, and investigate the motives of the many characters who inhabit traditional folklore.

EXPLORING POSSIBLE PREDICAMENTS IN IMAGINARY ROLE-PLAY AREAS

The teacher's involvement in role will establish the children's fictive world as something of value and importance and, by providing predicaments for the children to respond to, the teacher challenges the children to create stories. In addition, through entering the role-play area the teacher can deepen the imagined experience, question the learners, extend the role repertoire available to them, and join them in the active process of shaping, reshaping, exploring and experiencing the storydrama. In drama, participants agree:

> to suspend the reality of the classroom context in order to pretend, as a group, that they are *other* people in *another* place in *another* time.
>
> Neelands (1984)

Yet there will be no drama unless these young people in another place and time encounter problems or predicaments which they need to solve. Observing the children's play, the teacher can select a role to diversify the action. For example, the children's re-enactment of *Red Riding Hood* would be challenged by the arrival of their teacher in the forest as a lost rambler or a conservationist. The new character represents a structural problem for the children to solve. Will they alter the narrative, showing a flexible response, and weave the person into the tale? Will they dismiss the role? Or will they drop their tale and create a new one with this character? Such possibilities can be worked out together through improvisation and discussion.

Alternatively, the teacher can enter in role, present a problem to the children and leave them to deal with it, returning later to hear of their decisions or solutions. For example, the teacher might enter 'The magic garden of the elves' as an elf from the castle who is seeking the king's daughter. Can they help? Could a map of her favourite places in the garden be drawn? Are there any clues to be found? Professing the need to ask others, the teacher could leave, arranging to meet the 'elves' later.

Predicaments in role-play areas can also be seeded in written form, for example, postcards from the Giant noting his impending arrival, a hidden message from Friar Tuck warning of an ambush, an invitation from the Big Bad Wolf to a party, or a fairy note pinned to the door. However, mere information will not promote action and reflection; the teacher's written prompt needs to create some tension, or make explicit a conflict which could be followed up by her entry in role.

If the teacher provides time for groups to retell to the class the tales they have lived through in the area, then the stories that children create in these areas will seed other stories that their peers develop. 'Watch out!' Philip told Sean earnestly as his friend went towards the castle. 'The White Witch has stolen the king's keys and she's going to release the dragon!' There will also be informal retellings passed around, class anecdotes of 'lived' experience and subsequent playground re-enactments.

RESOURCE PROVISION IN IMAGINARY ROLE-PLAY AREAS

Resources can support and give focus to creative play and interest in the role-play area, and materials suggested and made by the children can enliven and redirect their improvisations. 'We need to make a golden egg, a giant one,' Samantha informed me. 'We're going to hide it!' In classrooms where personal and traditional tales are valued and shared, many children will request particular resources and use them imaginatively, allowing one prop to stand for another. While undertaking interior decorating in a castle with a group of five- to six-year-olds, Peter proposed creating paintings of the inhabitants, so portraits of characters were duly painted, labelled, framed and hung. Teachers and children can create lists of possible props which may trigger re-creations of tales and alternative versions.

PROPS AND RESOURCES FOR A CASTLE

crowns and gowns	bundle of straw
magic wand	single pea in a casket
treasure chest	royal stationery
silver slippers	map of kingdom
throne	wall mirror
coat of arms	portraits
spinning wheel	bag of gold

As children re-enact and explore a variety of tales in their castle area the range of resources used will widen, drawn from the world of folklore.

LANGUAGE LEARNING OPPORTUNITIES IN ROLE-PLAY AREAS

In successful role-play areas children do not make endless cups of tea but operate with conviction and concentration, challenged by problems encountered in this make-believe context. Imaginary role-play areas, when developed alongside a focus on storytelling in the classroom, can become creative contexts where stories are investigated and reworked, and the children's linguistic competence is extended. Frequently the children weave together a rich tapestry of tales, starting with one, meeting a character from another, finding common or new difficulties to deal with, and then illuminating the texts, the themes within the texts and the connections between the texts and their own lives. Encouraging children to use all the tales and texts they know enables them to develop their imaginative capacity. For in dramatic play situations like this, children try out various forms of spoken language in response to the demands of powerful and emotive predicaments. As Vygotsky (1978) noted, 'In play a child always behaves beyond his average age, above his daily behaviour...' The situation is fictional but their responses are real.

Real audiences for writing are found in abundance in this make-believe world and give focus and purpose to the children's writing. The teacher can prompt such writing and drawing, appearing in role, for example, as an editor of a local newspaper requesting news articles, as a wizard collecting new spells, or by simply providing a log book or diary for the characters to record their adventures. The children will also find their own reasons for writing, leaving codes for others to decipher, notes explaining their whereabouts, maps of the dungeons, diagrams of the undersea monsters that have been met, and so on. Natural environments such as forests and caves represent more of a challenge with regard to providing writing materials, although children frequently create a home base or a den in these areas and can carry paper and pencils in their rucksacks in order to leave messages on 'leaves' or carve signs into the 'rockface'.

Role-play areas can also be used to support story writing, since it allows them to live the story in a way which makes sense to them and then retell it in a pictorial sequence, or in words to the teacher scribe, so it can be recorded, re-read and retold.

In relation to reading, role-play areas can provide the context in which children are motivated to read – perhaps a letter, a map or note. In addition, the occasional class book, made retrospectively or as an ongoing text, which records the stories created in the role-play area, can become 'hot property'. Related traditional tale texts, too, become devourable literature when the role-play area is imaginary, since they provide more material for the children to experiment with and weave into their creative play. Obviously, teachers also need to read, share and tell appropriate stories to feed the story-making and storytelling process in the role-play area.

EXPLORING STORYTELLING AND DRAMA THROUGH PUPPETRY

Puppets can encourage children to tell and retell tales, tales which are frequently based on rich traditional recipes but may re-emerge through puppetry as a complex mix of the personal and traditional. Puppets can liberate children's voices, allowing them to explore different speech styles and registers, and play with a variety of intonations and language tunes. In giving the puppet a voice, the character comes to life, and enters and contributes to the unfolding narrative. So there are many opportunities for oral experimentation. Sometimes a narrator emerges in the group, prompting and occasionally controlling the action, but frequently this role is shared as the dramatic dialogue and story creation grow spontaneously. Alternatively, groups may plan their improvisation first and then re-create it. Clearly, both entrance points to the storytelling are valid and reflect the difference between spontaneous and prepared improvisation in drama.

There are a variety of ways to link storytelling, drama and puppetry. However, the discussion here is confined to the ways developed by a class of eight- to nine-year-olds who were working with home-made glove and finger puppets. A puppet theatre was made later in the work, but most of their imaginative retellings occurred in informal contexts in small groups without an audience. The puppets made were chosen from the following list that the children brainstormed.

POSSIBLE PUPPET CHARACTERS

frogs	princesses	dragons
giants	fairies	travellers
witches	kings	snakes
wizards	queens	knights
woodcutters	wolves	musicians
princes	fawns	beggars

Many of the puppets adopted particular character traits as a result of the physical features, facial expressions and clothes which they were given. Creating 'real' characters, and in some cases writing mini life histories for their puppets, strengthened the children's understanding of their characters' behaviour and views. 'We can't have your Princess Naomi in this,' announced Georgina. 'She wouldn't help the old traveller. She's never been kind to the poor before.'

A heated debate followed, led by the princess's creator who defended Princess Naomi and argued that she could be kind and caring. Eventually, the princess was given the role, and through the tale experienced the benefits of giving as well as receiving.

During the process of making their puppets, the children began to suggest and discuss various folk tales that they could perform, experimenting with dialogue and playing with different retellings. These informal discussions in small craft groups seeded most of the following activities, which different groups planned and developed together.

CREATING TALES WITH PARTICULAR CHARACTERS

Some children, working with their own puppets, created tales together in small groups. The improvisation, role-play and narrative were based on the interaction of the particular characters involved. For example, the tale of 'The Dog-eating Giant' emerged from the puppets of a king and queen, two dogs, a giant and a woodcutter. The greedy giant eventually got his deserved fate and ended up doing community service as an apprentice to the woodcutter, chewing down trees! The limited number of characters which the groups allowed themselves challenged them to create an inclusive story structure, and prompted the children to draw on tales known to them to create their own.

In another group the tale of 'The Frog Prince' was retold with a difference. A rogue snake puppet had to be woven into the tale, which created an intriguing challenge for the children, the snake causing problems in the princess's domestic life.

RECREATING KNOWN TALES

Several groups chose to retell a known traditional tale through narration and dialogue and borrowed other puppets to achieve this. Again, giving the group an additional and unlikely extra puppet character served to encourage more experimentation, different scenarios and sub-plots. However, in the main, these groups chose the security and comfort of revisiting their favourite folk tales and re-creating them together in their own words. Some groups retained silent puppets who merely mimed and moved, directed by the two or three narrators' voices, while other groups all took an active vocal part and the dialogue between characters became the main mode of storytelling. Others combined the voice of the unseen narrator and the voice of the characters. These imaginative re-creations gave the children the chance to explore different storytelling techniques. Relying upon the structure of a known tale allowed the children to experiment with voice play, with intonation and accents, humorous dialogue and dramatic exchanges.

REPLACING TALES

One group of children chose to replace their tale, prompting further adaptations. Their retelling of *The Three Little Pigs* living in an urban back street was an amusing parody, with the pigs as shady characters who wanted to build their houses in a public park. Mr Wilof, a local councillor, pursued them unmercifully in their illegal dealings. The physical construction of a town and park scenes, with the creative and conversational play which accompanied this, helped the children to establish their new version. Tony Ross's retelling of *The Three Little Pigs*, where his pigs find themselves on the thirty-ninth floor of a tower block, had probably influenced this alternative version, as in an early puppet session the group had decided to 'tell it differently', and Ross's book, which was known to them, had been re-read and enjoyed. Children who have told and retold tales orally are more confident to experiment with stories and to rework narratives for their own purposes.

PERFORMING TALES

The class worked for several weeks without a formal element of performance and then decided to plan a puppet show. With bamboo canes, lengths of wood, material and much design competence, the children built a basic puppet theatre. Programmes were compiled, seating plans were drawn, advertising posters pinned up and tickets issued. At this juncture more time for rehearsals was requested, and two groups decided to turn their tale into playscripts and learn the words. Prompters were engaged, although not eventually used, as the children continued to improvise and ad libbed around the story structure that they had created. The freedom to experiment with voices, change volume, pace and intonation, and playfully retell their tale through their puppets was seized upon and developed through the performances as well as through more informal puppet play, conferences and reflection.

Weeks later, several children chose to produce a written collection of the folk tales performed at the puppet show, retelling these tales as literary narratives with surprisingly little dialogue. So as with storydrama and role-play areas, puppetry fosters a multitude of storytelling and story-making opportunities which can be developed to imaginative advantage in the classroom.

HOW THE CRAB GOT ITS BACK
A Caribbean tale

There were once two sisters, Esmerelda and Yolanda, who were as different as chalk and cheese. You see, Esmerelda was plain (a sweet-natured girl she was, to be sure), but plain as plain can be. Yolanda, however, was a beauty. Her loveliness was arresting, her face shaped by luxurious curls, her skin flawless and her eyes inviting. But she was a proud and haughty girl, who expected much from those around her and gave little in return.

Yolanda would often instruct her sister to fetch and carry for her, to bake for her and to tend to the many chores that needed doing in their humble home. Esmerelda did as she bade. A sensitive sibling and dutiful daughter, she expected little from those around her but gave much in return.

One morning as I recall, Esmerelda was down by the river collecting water in large gourds for the family when she noticed an old woman sitting hunched up upon the river bank, with a cloth around her waist. She was trying to gather up handfuls of water to wash her back, but the liquid ran through her fingers as she sang in a tentative staccato voice:

> *Scratch my back daughter, oh*
> *Wash it well with water, oh.*

Esmerelda looked around to see if the old woman was referring to her. There was no one else about, so she listened again.

> *Scratch my back daughter, oh*
> *Wash it well with water, oh.*

She went over to the old woman and, using the water she'd collected in her gourds, she gently washed the old woman's back. It was red and sore, rough and raw, but every time Esmerelda paused, the old woman began to sing again, this time with more strength and insistence than before.

> *Scratch my back daughter, oh*
> *Wash it well with water, oh.*

The woman's skin felt as sharp as a prickly pear, and Esmerelda's hands began to bleed and her nails broke, yet still she continued to wash the woman's back. The old woman thanked Esmerelda. 'You are a good child,' she whispered. 'What do you wish for as your reward?'

'Oh, just your blessing, mother,' replied Esmerelda, expecting little else.

'Then, my child, look deep into the water and you shall see what you will be.'

Esmerelda bent over the water and looked into the dark face of the river. Its depths were cloudy, but as they cleared she saw staring back at her, open-mouthed and wide-eyed, the gentle face of a very beautiful girl; her soul had surfaced and its beauty shone for all to see. She turned to thank the woman, but strangely she was nowhere to be seen.

Esmerelda, amazed and delighted, danced back towards the village, but when Yolanda saw her she could scarcely believe her jealous eyes. She demanded an explanation, but did not wait to hear the full story, and rushed down to the river bank, her head bursting with her own desires. Impatient to find the source of her sister's good fortune, she rushed past an old woman who sat hunched on the river bank singing.

Scratch my back daughter, oh
Wash it well with water, oh.

Yolanda looked at the old woman whose hands and feet seemed shrivelled and bent, and whose back was so criss-crossed and cracked it looked red and sore, and heard the words again:

Scratch my back daughter, oh
Wash it well with water, oh.

'Oh for goodness sake,' Yolanda snapped at the figure. 'Don't bother me now. Can't you see I'm busy?'

Scratch my back daughter, oh
Wash it well with water, oh.

'I've told you,' insisted Yolanda. 'I've got far more important things to do than help you. Scratch it yourself with those claws of yours, you ugly, old creature.'

'Insolent girl!' denounced the old woman in a sinister whisper. 'As you see me, so shall you be.'

At that moment Yolanda began to change – to shrink, to shake, to shriek, to shiver. Her slender arms and legs shrank and shrank, and became hard and clawlike. Her head sunk into her torso and her inviting eyes peered out of the crisp carapace of the shell which now encompassed her.

So it was that the Crab got its back and began its hermit-like existence. Such crabs cannot bear to be seen, knowing that they were once beautiful. They hide in hollows, in rock pools and under stones, and when sand fills their cracks and their backs itch they are forced to crawl down into the water to wash it off, for no one will scratch their backs for them.

CHAPTER 5

PLANNING TRADITIONAL STORYTELLING IN THE CURRICULUM

In an already packed curriculum, implementing traditional storytelling may initially appear to be a challenge. However, storytelling work in the classroom involves not only the oral retelling of tales but also reading, writing and drama. It can also prompt creative responses in art, dance and music as well as links with other curriculum areas such as history and religious education. To harness the potential of storytelling, this work needs to be planned across the school and informed by national curricula and guidelines. Teachers can either create their own plans for blocked units of work from the frameworks described in this chapter, or integrate oral storytelling into ongoing English work in some of the ways detailed here. Assessment opportunities within this language work will also need to be identified and related to the school's assessment and recording policy.

PLANNING STORYTELLING INTO CONTINUING WORK

Teachers who have become confident as storytellers find that oral storytelling is an invaluable tool in the ongoing classroom context. So, too, is knowledge of a range of folk and fairy tales, myths and legends. A commitment to a blocked unit of work can provide focused development time, but the skills, knowledge and understanding about language, developed through this work, can be usefully revisited and consolidated through ongoing work.

In terms of reading, traditional tales represent an explicit resource. In many schools a book box of multicultural tales and tapes travel the classes to widen the range of literature available. This provides extra material for silent reading time and, if booked for a week or more, can enable the teacher to plan additional language work, selecting from the storytelling activities described in Chapters 3 and 4, and developing children's responses to literature and written narrative competence.

Anthologies of folk tales also lend themselves to group reading as the short story format is both accessible and appropriate. Additionally, integrating oral stories into the planned 'read aloud' programme ensures that there is variety in both content and delivery. Establishing a routine for the oral storytelling part of this programme is useful, and may involve telling only a small section from a story each day. This limits the task for a novice storyteller and prompts the children to predict and discuss the unfolding tale.

Time to reflect upon the retold tales must be planned into storytime, to help children develop their insights and understanding. The quality of this informal interaction about the story is significant, and a battery of teacher questions are to be avoided. In pairs, children can share their perceptions and then respond to issues raised, in a collective reconstruction of the layers in the story.

In relation to ongoing speaking and listening activities, offering informal opportunities for sharing personal stories as well as traditional tales can easily be part of the regular provision of oral work. Newstime in many classrooms has been replaced by a sharing circle when, among other activities, narratives from home, from the media and the playground are shared. Retelling traditional tales in this story circle, or in a weekly 'tales for the telling' time is also possible.

Role-play areas of both the functional and imaginary kind also provide contexts in which storytelling and story making can be developed, as does regular classroom drama. The production of radio plays and programmes, documentaries, story tapes, puppet shows, performance drama and so on will also involve different forms of speaking and listening, including storytelling and a variety of forms of related reading and writing.

Nancy Martin (1976) argued, 'Reading and writing float on a sea of talk' and since narrative is an accessible form of talking and thinking, it should be harnessed more rigorously as a resource in planning and developing the whole curriculum. Teachers can make frequent use of children's oral narrative competence in many subjects: in historical re-creations, as a form of reporting back in science, in the context of visits and trips, and in mathematical enquiries. Indeed, the provision of opportunities to develop and use communication skills by presenting ideas, explaining results, and reporting to a range of audiences is central to national curricula requirements and guidelines in science and mathematics. Such activities rely implicitly on spoken narrative and help children to make full use of this powerful medium for organising and understanding experience. The frequent use of oral narrative in these curriculum contexts will help to establish a storytelling ethos in the classroom which can be extended through blocked work.

PLANNING TRADITIONAL STORYTELLING PROJECTS AND DEVELOPED UNITS OF WORK

Projects or units of work on storytelling can focus explicitly on the development of oral work while also acting as a rich resource for developing key skills in reading and writing. Adopting such a focus ensures that oral work is planned for and features as a distinct component in the year's plan.

Across the primary school, blocked units of work on traditional storytelling can respond to curriculum requirements and provide both continuity and progression. Many year groups plan for a biannual focus on storytelling, ensuring that young children who have been introduced to a range of traditional tales and have developed their strengths as storytellers can extend their language competence in this area. Blocked units of work may last any length of time, from a fortnight to half a term or more, and may take a particular focus, selected perhaps from the different genre within the oral tradition (fables or fairy tales, tall tales or folk tales, myths or legends, family histories or local legends). Alternatively, teachers may select particular tales which focus on personal, social and emotional issues (fear of the unknown, love and hate, family loyalties). Equally, a more eclectic mix of stories can be used for a storytelling project. The selection will always depend on the learning objectives identified for the work. It may be appropriate that breadth and knowledge of a range of stories is the initial concern in the early years, while knowledge of particular kinds of traditional tales enhance the middle years, and increased variety and challenge are targeted in the upper primary years.

Storytelling projects may well be linked to other curriculum work. For example, family stories may tie into an early years focus on ourselves and our past. Local history studies may prompt investigation and research into legendary local characters, real and fictional. Religious beliefs and habits may be better understood through storydrama investigations. History and geography work can focus on the knowledge about lifestyles, customs and societies which can be gained through a culture's stories. Alternatively, a traditional storytelling focus may represent the main body of English work and operate independently of other subjects.

Teachers planning a blocked unit of storytelling work will need to consider the following:
✧ What are the overall aims of this work?
✧ What curriculum areas could be integrated into this work?
✧ What particular sub-focus/theme would suit the work?
✧ Are the resource collections of tales and tapes adequate?
✧ What other resources does the project require?
✧ Would a visiting storyteller aid this work?
✧ How often will the class work on this project?
✧ What organisational groupings would be most helpful?
✧ What practical strategies and elements of performance will help the children develop as storytellers?
✧ How is the work to be recorded/assessed?
✧ How will the children reflect on their storytelling?

✧ What event might the class work towards?

✧ What balance should be planned between reading and writing, speaking and listening?

Consideration of such issues will shape the work on traditional storytelling. The four examples of blocked units of English work outlined below were planned and undertaken by different teachers and serve to provide possible frameworks for discussion and extrapolation.

EXAMPLE 1: STORYTELLING – ANIMAL FOLK TALES

This unit of work was developed in a class of five- to six-year-olds across a four-week period. It aimed to introduce children to a number of animal tales, to examine the characters portrayed in these tales and to use puppets to aid the retellings.

PREPARATORY ACTIVITIES

✧ Teacher told a variety of animal tales.

✧ Children responded to these through drawing, talking and writing.

✧ Class created a display of animals in folk tales.

MAIN DEVELOPMENT WORK

✧ Teacher told several different folk tales about two types of animal (wolves and frogs).

✧ Children focused on the actions and attitudes of these animal characters in the different tales.

✧ Simple puppets were made and used for informal retellings of the tales.

✧ Children received a letter from the Big Bad Wolf and engaged in storydrama and writing.

✧ Class performed puppet retellings to parents and siblings.

EXTENSION AND REVIEW

✧ Class collected story books about animals and categorised these tales (scary tales, humorous tales and so on).

✧ Class reported on this work in assembly.

RESOURCES

A selection of animal folk tales in picture-book retellings; junk materials for making puppets.

EXAMPLE 2: STORYTELLING – FOLK AND FAIRY TALES

This unit of English work was undertaken with a class of six- to seven-year-olds across a six-week period. It aimed to widen children's knowledge of traditional folk and fairy tales, to extend their confidence as storytellers to different audiences and to examine different versions of the same story. The class appeared to feel that there were correct and incorrect versions of tales and their teacher wished to dispel this myth.

PREPARATORY ACTIVITIES

✦ Teacher and children shared personal and family stories.
✦ Teacher told a variety of folk and fairy tales.
✦ Class retold and rewrote tales in pairs and in the class story circle.
✦ Class brainstormed known folk and fairy tales.
✦ Traditional tale texts promoted in quiet reading time.

MAIN DEVELOPMENT WORK

✦ Role-play area established as 'The land of fairy tales'.
✦ Storydrama to investigate 'The land of fairy tales'.
✦ Children selected a particular tale to work on.
✦ Activities to support remembering the tale.
✦ Practice and preparation for performance.
✦ An afternoon of storytelling – pairs retold tales to groups in a parallel class.

EXTENSION AND REVIEW

✦ Reviewed the storytelling afternoon.
✦ Examined different children's book versions of *The Three Little Pigs* and *Jack and the Beanstalk*.
✦ Wrote and illustrated new retellings for the class anthology, many of which had been created in the storydrama.

RESOURCES

A selection of picture-book retellings of folk and fairy tales; different written versions of the same story; equipment, curtains, scenery and props for the role-play area; cassette recorders and audio cassettes.

EXAMPLE 3: STORYTELLING – MYTHS AND LEGENDS

This unit of work was undertaken across a half-term by two classes of eight- to nine-year-olds. It aimed to extend the children's knowledge and understanding of myths and legends and other cultures, and to link this work to storydrama and the visual arts, as well as involve parents.

PREPARATORY ACTIVITIES

✧ Two teachers told a variety of myths and legends and swapped classes to share these.

✧ Each class located the parts of the world from where the stories originated – a corporate display was made.

✧ Each class were encouraged to read myths and legends and bring such books in from home.

✧ The common elements in myths and legends were identified.

MAIN DEVELOPMENT WORK

✧ Telling and retelling activities (spoken and written) centred upon the origin of myths.

✧ Storydrama sessions examined such myths and built new myths from story fragments.

✧ Related RE and geography work undertaken.

✧ Parents invited into a joint class 'Parents as storytellers' afternoon where some shared personal stories and myths or legends from their own culture.

✧ Groups selected a myth to explore through art and craft, music, dance and drama (using the particular talents of both teachers).

✧ Each group prepared and shared an artistic performance of their chosen myth with groups from the parallel class.

EXTENSION AND REVIEW

✧ Children composed and published their own origin of myths, or contemporary myths/legends about the local area.
✧ Classes presented their work, stories and tapes in assembly.

RESOURCES

A selection of myths and legends from many cultures; a world map; resources for art/craft/music; cassette recorders and audio cassettes.

EXAMPLE 4: STORYTELLING –
STYLES AND TRADITIONS

This unit of work was undertaken over a half-term by three classes of ten- to eleven-year-olds in one school. It aimed to extend the children's knowledge of the different styles and traditions of storytelling, to examine characters and to help the children develop their own storytelling techniques.

PREPARATORY ACTIVITIES

✧ Teachers told a variety of traditional tales.
✧ Children listed and categorised known tales.
✧ Children identified expectations with regard to characters and heroes/heroines.
✧ Children/teacher read modernised retellings and tales with alternative gender roles.

MAIN DEVELOPMENT WORK

✧ Children worked on tales, telling, writing and experimenting.
✧ A visiting Indian storyteller ran workshops in each class.
✧ Children discussed storytelling styles and features of performance using audio cassettes and a video of the storyteller.
✧ Each child prepared to retell a chosen tale.
✧ Children refined their performance skills through taped drafts and storytelling conferences.
✧ Each class visited younger classes as 'the storytellers' in the school's book week.

EXTENSION AND REVIEW

✧ Children reviewed their storytelling in learning logs and discussed skills gained.

✧ Each child changed the genre and rewrote their chosen tale as a news article, poem, playscript, etc.

✧ One class created a story tape and sold copies.

RESOURCES

The visiting storyteller; a selection of traditional tale texts; cassette recorders and audio cassettes.

In all these examples of extended storytelling work a central concern was the children being the oral storytellers and widening their repertoire of stories. All classes also worked towards an event or a storytelling afternoon which gave their work a genuine urgency and purpose and a real audience with whom to share their stories. In most classes a final written or taped anthology was produced. This is a useful by-product and evidence of the oral work undertaken but by no means essential. Each project offered the teachers many opportunities to assess children's speaking and listening in a variety of social contexts and in individual, pair, group and whole-class settings.

STORYTELLING EVENTS AND FESTIVALS

To give traditional tales and their telling a higher profile for children, teachers, parents, governors and in the wider community, storytelling events and festivals can be invaluable. They can tie together a variety of classroom practices, and create opportunities to involve parents and inform them about the role of storytelling in the development of language and literacy. Such events can also provide multiple audiences and help children to establish a sense of themselves as part of a community of storytellers.

Initially it may be easier to organise a one-day event, with a visiting storyteller, teachers exchanging classes to retell their favourite tales, and children pairing for an oral story swap.

If more time is available, a week-long educational extravaganza could be planned that celebrates storytelling and storydrama. This might be for the whole school or for a particular year group, offering extensive opportunities for children to operate as storytellers. Such an event can give tremendous momentum to integrated language practice, raise the status of traditional storytelling and engender enthusiasm and interest in this earliest form of education.

As with all such events, prior preparation in terms of work undertaken in classrooms, and planned follow-up, can make a significant difference to its long-term educational impact. A festival can act as a finale or celebration at the close of a unit of work or as an enriching stimulus which builds on previous work and encourages extension activities. A theme or title may help to provide the programme of events with coherence. Examples include 'Heroes and heroines', 'Animal tales', 'Multicultural stories', 'Tales of magic, mystery and wonder', 'Tales from the Far East' and 'Tales: ancient and modern'. In organising such an event some of the following tried and tested suggestions could be employed.

INVITE A PROFESSIONAL OR A LOCAL STORYTELLER

Their finely honed skills may well seed work right across the curriculum for several weeks afterwards. The Society for Storytelling (SfS) publishes a directory of storytellers (see page 165) with names, addresses and a summary of individual skills and experience in educational settings, but personal recommendations are also worth seeking. There is an enormous wealth of professional talent available to schools, and considerable cultural diversity in styles and traditions practised. Perhaps the school could even consider a residency. Regional arts associations may be able to give advice on seeking additional funding.

Local librarians often have considerable experience of telling stories to groups of children and, like parents, classroom assistants and members of the local community, they represent a resource in storytelling events.

ORGANISE STORYTELLING SESSIONS AND SWAPS

Various kinds of storytelling sessions can be planned to ensure that everyone in the school/year group is given the chance to be an official storyteller during the festival, preferably to children not in their class. This is a central feature of any storytelling festival which should provide a range of audiences and contexts, both informal and formal, in which children (individually and in pairs and groups) share and perform their chosen tales. Children are all storytellers and need to be given the chance to take a full part in this oral tradition. The use of curtain material over school chairs, props and token costumes can enhance the status of the young storytellers in a 'Talk Story Festival'. The range of styles previously explored by classes can be celebrated and shared. This may involve groups in creating puppet shows, using dance, drama or songs in their stories or enhancing their performance with music and percussion. Many others will share their tale through spoken word and gesture alone.

PLAN STORY-BASED ARTS WORKSHOPS

Each member of staff could plan a folklore-related workshop. These could include art and craft sessions, mask making, puppetry, story quilts (see page 63), dance, drama and creative writing, and build on staff interest and expertise. Through repeating such sessions, younger and older children can be catered for and challenged accordingly. The festival's theme will be a springboard for planning these workshops.

PLAN A 'PARENTS ARE STORYTELLERS' AFTERNOON

This could be incorporated within the festival week and involve a number of parents coming to share their personal stories or favourite oral stories with groups of children. Time needs to be provided for children to tell their prepared tales within these small story circles too. In one school, the twenty parents who joined in a 'Parents tell stories' afternoon put up a list of the titles of the tales they planned to tell before the event and children signed up for their choice (some of which were told in different languages).

PROFILE STORYTELLING IN ASSEMBLIES

These communal contexts provide an excellent opportunity for sharing and celebrating the many activities undertaken during the 'Talk Story Festival'. In addition, each member of staff could share a brief personal story and display an object reminiscent of her anecdote. A teachers' 'Tales from home' display in the hall can become a simple yet fascinating focus at the start of a festival. Each assembly will provide the children with the chance to hear another teacher's tale. Stories breed stories and such events will foster listening and learning about others. A display of 'story objects' could also be used in the classroom to promote the sharing of personal stories during story-circle time.

PROMOTE STORYTELLING THROUGH DISPLAYS

Although this is essentially an oral art form, there are many visual ways to convey its significance. Photographs of the children engaged in telling stories and in storydrama can be displayed with links to relevant national curricula or current guidelines to point out the breadth of work involved. A world map with arrows and titles indicating the probable countries of origin can highlight diversity, and surveys of children's favourite folk tales, myths and legends can be wall mounted as well as their story quilts. Artwork inspired by stories can also be displayed.

PRODUCE STORYTELLING TAPES

It is a worthwhile venture to create an edited school story tape with tales told by children from each class. The variety of voices and different kinds of story productions will make this a rich resource, a copy of which can be added to each class's audio-cassette collection or even sold to parents. The inlay cards can be designed by the children and include information about the tales and the storytellers. Such story tapes offer another vehicle to promote the power, potential and creativity of the spoken word.

ORGANISE A BOOKSHOP

This could offer a range of anthologies, multicultural tales, audio cassettes, picture-book retellings and contemporary parodies of well-known tales. Some of the stories recommended in Appendix 1 (see pages 165–79) could be requested. Texts with riddles, rhymes, jokes and rhythms, also part of the oral tradition of folklore, would widen the selection for sale.

ORGANISE A STORYTELLING WORKSHOP FOR ADULTS

Working with a group of volunteers (parents, governors, members of the local community) during the storytelling festival can highlight the ageless nature of this art form, and give these adults more confidence to tell and retell stories both in the home and in the classroom context. The local library may be able to organise such an event.

ORGANISE A COMMUNITY STORYTELLING EVENT

An after-school story hour open to parents, siblings, nursery children and local youth associations could be planned. Starting with a communal joining-in story, this could move on to story-based activities and group retellings. Organising an evening of storytelling for the community, with children, teachers and others telling stories, is also very worthwhile, since oral stories can build bonds, bridge gaps and bring people together.

SUPPORTING STAFF DEVELOPMENT

In schools where only a few staff are confident storytellers and where the children are not offered opportunities to engage in traditional storytelling projects, a festival or single storytelling event may be particularly helpful to develop staff interest and enthusiasm, although if teachers wish to extend this work in their classrooms then further professional development opportunities and in-service training may be needed. For as Stenhouse (1975) observed, 'There is no curriculum development without staff development.' Teachers need to be convinced of the educational value of storytelling and to become acquainted with a range of practical classroom strategies which can help children develop as storytellers and story makers. In addition, teachers need to engage in oral storytelling themselves and encounter the pleasure, creativity and challenge which the oral tradition offers.

Confidence as a storyteller grows with experience and through support. The strategies detailed in the following chapter may help teachers develop a sense of security, extend their memory and release their artistic energy and potential. In fact, a number of the activities in Chapters 3, 4 and 6 could be used for staff meetings and development days to involve staff in retelling tales and help them consider the value of planning storytelling into the curriculum. Further ideas include the following.

✧ Share personal stories and discuss the use of narrative as a form of thinking, and as a tool for organising experience in both home and school contexts.

✧ Reflect upon the current opportunities for storytelling offered in the curriculum. Could these be expanded?

✧ Listen to children's taped retellings and consider the learning about language involved.

✧ Brainstorm known traditional tales. What does the breadth and diversity indicate?

✧ Retell some of these tales in pairs or groups and discuss the nature of the task and the story themes.

✧ Invite in a professional storyteller/educator to share strategies, ideas and stories.

✧ Examine the resources currently available in the school, and devise a plan for their improved use.

✧ Plan together, in pairs, year groups or as a staff, to raise the profile of oral storytelling in the school, and to document, review and record the children's progress.

Through profiling traditional storytelling in school, and sharing the learning opportunities offered and the work undertaken, integrated and exciting language practices can be planned which revolve around this ancient form of education.

HOW THE SUN CAME INTO THE WORLD
An Australasian tale

In the dream-time, before men came into the world, there was no sun – only the distant moon – and the birds and animals had to creep about as best they could among the shadows and the darkness. The animals did not complain for they knew of no alternative, but there were many accidents as the animals bumped into one another, trod on one another and crept cautiously about, peering warily into the inky blackness.

One day, on the edge of the plains of the Murrumbidgee River, Dineewan the Emu and the Brolga fell to fierce fighting. Their quarrel could be heard by all around as it echoed up the valley. Screeching at each other in anger, Brolga suddenly lunged forward and, seizing one of the Emu's huge eggs, hurled it with all her might up into the dark sky. Up and up it soared, up past the thick cloud layer, up into the infinite space beyond. There it fell upon a pile of firewood, burst its yolk and set light to the kindling. The fire blazed in the sky and the animals below were amazed, their eyes dazzled by its light. For the first time they could see each other clearly; for the first time they could view the world around them; for the first time they could move with confidence. They looked and looked. Some began to explore their new environment, while others basked in the warmth thrown down by the roaring flames. All too soon, however, the fire in the sky burned out and the earth and all its creatures returned to the vast unknowing darkness of before.

Now a kindly Sky Spirit had watched the animals and seen their pleasure. He could also foresee some of the benefits of light on earth, and he determined to try to light a new fire. All that night the Sky Spirit and his many helpers worked in the heavens gathering wood, and when the next day was due to begin the Spirit made ready to light the fire. Wisely he sent the Morning Star to shine on the animals and warn them that the fire was about to be lit, so that they would not be afraid when the flames crackled and light dawned. But very few creatures were awake to notice the Morning Star gleaming in the sky. Most of the animals and birds remained in deep slumber.

So the Sky Spirit turned to Gougourhgah the Kookaburra, and asked him if he would await the sign from the Morning Star that the fire was about to be lit and then awaken the animals with his loud and braying call. Gougourhgah was well pleased with this honour. He sat on a branch of an old gum tree, opened his beak and called 'Gou gour gah ghah, Gou gour gah ghah, Gou gour gah ghah!'

Every single creature nestled asleep on the plains beside the Murrumbidgee River awoke, and the great fire in the sky was kindled. Throughout the morning the fire burned brighter and brighter, and as midday approached the flames grew hotter and hotter, sending much light and intense heat to the earth below.

Towards the close of the day the strength of the fire abated, and the red and golden rays of the very first sunset were seen. The wise Sky Spirit wrapped the dying embers of the fire in clouds and preserved them until the very next morning, when he used them to light another fire.

Indeed, as far as I know, he has continued doing so from that day to this. As for the Kookaburra, he continues to call 'Gou gour gah ghah, Gou gour gah ghah, Gou gour gah ghah!' before each dawn, and when man came to inhabit the earth he learned to honour the great Kookaburra who welcomed the sun each morning. Children were forbidden to laugh at the Kookaburra's big mouth and strident call.

'For if you insult Gougourhgah the Kookaburra,' their parents told them, 'then he may take offence and not greet the sun for us each day.'

It is said that if the children defied their parents and poked fun at the Kookaburra's braying laugh, then an extra tooth would grow near their eye-teeth. They were then disfigured and lost their beauty, and everyone knew they had laughed at Gougourhgah the Kookaburra who brought the sun into the world. 'Gou gour gah ghah, Gou gour gah ghah, Gou gour gah ghah!'

CHAPTER 6

SUPPORTING TEACHERS AS STORYTELLERS

Humans are natural tellers of tales. Friends share anecdotes of everyday living, relatives recall family folklore, and everyone reflects upon the past and anticipates the future in words and thoughts shaped as stories.

However, not everyone has the confidence to tell stories to large groups of listeners, to a class, to the staff or to the school in assembly. Initially new tellers may feel nervous and insecure yet are frequently surprised at the ease with which the words begin to flow, the striking rapport that is established with the audience and the intense pleasure and satisfaction that storytelling can bring. Teachers, in developing their confidence as storytellers, can lean on the accessible nature of narrative, their wealth of experience of retelling personal anecdotes and their often unacknowledged imaginative capacity.

There is no blueprint for becoming a storyteller. Storytellers are not necessarily performers or dramatists but sharers of tales conveyed through the spoken word. In fact, there are as many ways to tell stories as there are people to tell them. Individuals will develop their own style, refine their skills and release their creative potential through the enjoyment of the process of telling tales, and then retelling them.

SELECTING TALES FOR THE TELLING

Teachers new to storytelling sometimes prefer to begin by telling stories from their own childhood to small groups of children. Personal tales are easier to recall, although adaptations and embellishments appropriate for telling to a young audience may need to be considered. Memories of significant events offer the class an insight into their teacher's life and will prompt children to share their personal and family stories also.

However, the main source of material for storytellers are the myths, legends, folk and fairy tales of multicultural society, many of which lend themselves to being told, not read. Children need to encounter a range of literature in school from a variety of literary traditions and cultures; in selecting traditional tales to tell from many different cultures the teacher can be sure that a real diversity of literature is experienced. The wealth of material available to choose from, however, can be overwhelming, so selecting an anthology, taped collection, or single picture book recommended in Appendix 1 (see pages 165–79), or reading the traditional tales retold in this book, will represent a first step towards selection. It is also worthwhile seeking opportunities to hear experienced storytellers as their tales can expand the teacher's repertoire. Told tales are often easier to remember and retell.

The importance of finding short tales which have an instinctive and immediate appeal should not be underestimated. The most successful stories are those which have real meaning and significance for the teller, since unless the tale is in tune with the teller it will not work well. A teacher's enthusiasm for a story is infectious. It allows the story to be 'sung' creatively and fosters commitment from the audience, enticing them to listen, wonder, feel and respond. Teachers working to a tight timetable may need to search for tales for particular purposes: to enrich cross-curricular work, to examine moral values and practices, and to highlight commonalities and differences across time and between cultures. Traditional tales open doors into the arts, the sciences and the humanities, but such doors must not be forced open at the expense of losing the teacher's interest in and critical commitment to the tale. Finding tales that are waiting to be told, that the storyteller really wants to share, for whatever conscious or unconscious reason, remains important. The hunt is not a quick or easy one, but it is always worth the journey.

Following the selection of a possible tale, it is useful to re-read it several times, to identify and absorb its layers and locate areas of personal interest or intrigue. Certain tales have the power and energy to attract readers straight back to them and demand to be told, while other tales may be read or heard and revisited later, waiting their turn to be selected as appropriate for a particular purpose or audience. Some traditional tales, through translation or being written down, have lost their distinctly oral flavour, their immediacy, directness and strong sense of rhythm, but some tellers will prefer to prepare more literary prose to tell.

LEARNING THE TALE

Storytelling does not require word-for-word recall; indeed, rote memorisation plays little or no part in this art form. As the story is retold, there will be many subtle changes, minor alterations and perhaps major remouldings which emerge. Some of these will have been carefully considered, while others will appear at the very moment of telling and be built upon by the storyteller. Some changes may alter the tale fundamentally, while others will only make small differences to the story. Each retelling, however, will be utterly unique, a re-creation full of feeling and creative energy, but based substantially upon the tale.

> I think stories must be acquired by long contemplation, by bringing the imagination to work, constantly, intelligently upon them. And finally by that power to blow the breath of life into them. And the method? That of learning incident by incident, or picture by picture. Never word by word.
>
> Sawyer (1962)

To retell the tale, the teacher will need to become well acquainted with it, to learn the shape of the tale and make choices about any planned changes. Once the general shape of the story has been committed to memory, in words or pictures, then the teacher will be more confident to retell the tale creatively. However, while changes are inevitable, teachers need not feel pressured to alter the tale, only encouraged to make it theirs in whatever way suits them. This imitative reproduction process is itself an active and creative one, as Cassirer (1953) has argued, and is a crucial feature of the oral tradition.

Many traditional tales have similar story shapes and patterns which make them easier to recall. Frequently, such tales are moulded for the ear, and include some repetition, a clear rhythmic quality and memorable language. All these features help to fix the tale in the mind of the teller. However, the overall story shape is significant, and several different strategies can be used to help the storyteller learn this.

The story structure can be analysed, if the story is a straightforward one, and broken down into its component parts: the beginning, the sequence of significant events which represent the middle, and the end. These parts can be recorded on a postcard in note form, or in pictures as a memory map to support recall. This card prompt could be placed nearby during a storytelling in case of emergencies.

The backbone of the story can be recorded as a keyword summary, an ordered list, and memory aid. (See the keyword summary on page 66.) During the live performance the storyteller puts flesh upon the backbone of the tale through her language, intonation, gestures and emotive re-creation, but the backbone remains a fairly constant structure, an unchanging sequence.

A series of images from the story can be identified by the storyteller. These pictures are brought to life in the mind's eye and painted verbally during the retelling. Using this strategy the tale is learned through visual recall of significant events, characters' facial expressions, the physical environment and so on, as these are seen in the storyteller's imagination. Investigating where a story is set and how it relates to its culture of origin can develop a more accurate, less stereotypical painting. Alternatively, the teller may replace the tale in a setting well known to her and subtly alter the tale through this personal connection and replacement.

The major scenes in the story can be drawn in strict sequential order and labelled to secure these as landmarks in the mind of the teller. These comic strips can become useful memory maps. Recalling sensory aspects of the scenes – the elements of smell, sound, sight, taste and touch – can also aid the spoken evocation and description.

A photocopy of the tale can enable the storyteller to work on the story shape: to divide the tale into chunks, subtitle sections, highlight figurative phrases and draw pictures or make notes in the margin. Similarly, printed illustrations from tales can help to fix specific features or visuals in the mind. Such written responses, plans and notes can aid recall of the shape and provide the security to prompt expansion.

Each storyteller will learn to remember the story structure in different ways, but once the overall shape of the story is anchored securely in their mind, particular attention can be paid to specific language features, which the storyteller may wish to retain within their telling. Notes can be made of common phrases, runs and repetitions, Homeric epithets (for example, 'wine-dark sea') and rhymes or songs which contribute to the effectiveness of the tale. For instance, in *How the Tides came to Ebb and Flow* (see pages 5–7) the prayers of the old woman and the songs and callings of the Great Sea Bird and the Little Rainbow Fish are worth memorising accurately or creating one's own version. These can be committed to a storyteller's notebook as a permanent record. Particularly evocative words or lyrical phrases are also worth noting if they enhance the spirit of the tale.

The beginnings and endings of tales can also be valuably recorded. Storytellers may choose to retell the story from a different place within the tale, and noting this with a few starting words or phrases will help to set the scene and provide confidence in establishing the tone of the tale. There are many traditional beginnings and endings to tales which have over the centuries been created to draw the audience into the world of story and to release them into the real world afterwards. These travel from one story to another and are timeless formulae from the oral tradition. For example:

Beginnings

✧ Snip, snap, chin, my story's in...

✧ It wasn't in my time and it wasn't in your time, but it was in somebody's time...

✧ It was in the place where North, South, East and West meet...

✧ There was, there was not...

✧ In the time when birds made nests in old men's beards...

✧ In the time before time began...

✧ Once there was, and once there was not...

✧ Now I shall light the story fire; the flame will burn brightly; beware...

Endings

✧ Snip, snap, snout, my story's out.

✧ And so it was until this day, unless that is you know differently.

✧ My tale I have told it,
In your bosom now hold it.

✧ We have travelled from mountain to mountain,
We have travelled from wood to wood,
I have heard this story from good folk
And have told it to folk who are good.

✧ Three apples fell from heaven:
One for the teller,
One for the listener
And one for the one who heard.

✧ A story, a story. Let it come. Let it go.

✧ And that's the way it was, and that's the way it is to this good day.

✧ The flames are dying down now, but the story's embers will glow in our minds for ever and always.

A storyteller's notebook or file is one way to retain such phrases. This is simply a permanent condensed collection of known tales, story shapes, particular language features, source notes and other relevant information. It can enable the teller to revisit old favourites years later and to recall and retell them. Notebooks often become indispensable as memory prompts, and precious and well-worn possessions as records of the teller's expanding repertoire.

All the hard work on story shape, investigating the story, or recording summaries in notebooks to aid memory retention will be of little value, however, without serious practice. Practice in telling the tale is vital to learn it and to own the story. Telling and retelling the tale to different people, to oneself or on to tape can increase the teller's power of recall, sense of security and confidence. As Eileen Colwell, an experienced storyteller, comments:

> Practice and experience enable the storyteller to bring out the full potential of a story.
>
> Colwell (1991)

The flavour, feel and temperature of a tale and any possible changes can all be embedded in a telling through practice, preparation and the experience of telling and retelling the tale.

STRATEGIES TO SUPPORT THE TELLING

Some professional storytellers develop and refine a particular style of storytelling, learned early within their culture; others experiment with various styles according to the tale chosen. Novice storytellers should consider what feels comfortable to them, find a place on the continuum of storytellers whose styles range from simply sharing a story in an undemonstrative 'low-key' way to a very dramatic live performance. Somewhere in the middle of the continuum lies a more collaborative style of telling which encourages active audience participation: the central storyteller invites the audience not only to join in choruses but also to fill gaps, solve problems and co-create the tale in words. However, there is tremendous variety even within a single tradition as the teller's style will be partly influenced by each tale and audience. The emotional temperature of a tale and the themes it examines often suggest a particular style of telling. For example, *The Children of Wax* (see pages 56–7) lends itself to a quieter more reflective delivery than the action-packed story *The End of Baba Yaga* (see pages 31–2).

Deciding how to tell a tale, how to interpret it and how to share it will be a personal matter, but Betty Rosen offers good advice when she notes:

> ...if I thoroughly digest the story I will discover my dominant feelings about it. Wrapping these feelings around key moments, I find that the means of the retelling comes of itself...To have authenticity means to be fair to both the story itself and one's own response to it: these should dictate the mode of telling.
>
> B. Rosen (1993)

Storytellers employ numerous skills to assist the telling and create their style. These skills are used in different measures in response to different tales and include pace, voice play, eye contact, gesture, visual aids, artefacts, music, rhythm and so on. However, it is the story that really counts; the power of the tale itself will work on the audience. The storyteller simply selects ways to embellish or intensify the tale through her use of some features of performance. All storytellers can refine their verbal and non-verbal skills through reflection and practice. This simply requires a commitment to voice and body play, to trialling, experimenting and feeling the effect of various components and selecting those most suitable to the tale and the chosen style of telling.

Pacing the tale in response to the shape of the story is essential. Novice storytellers may wish to plan for this, but tellers will find that pace and pauses for dramatic effect emerge naturally by 'living through' the tale as it is told. Speed can be used to highlight action sections, whereas a particularly poignant section may respond to a slower, more lyrical delivery. Repetitive phrases, refrains, chants or songs can be given pace according to their meaning and rhythm; the same rhythm and pace needs to be retained for these repetitions throughout.

Using pauses to create tension, build anticipation, mark a moment or divide sections of the tale is an effective device and a valuable skill. For example, in the tale *Ladder to the Sky* (see pages 11–12) there is a section where discontent begins to grow. This section could be spoken quickly (as if the words offer a bad taste in the mouth), making an effective contrast with the following potentially slow and melancholic scene, which describes the young man's departure and his grandmother's loss. A lengthy pause could be taken when the grandmother reaches the top of the vine to prompt prediction and add significance to her action.

There is no need to rush; rather the expectant pause, packed with prediction, can be savoured by the storyteller and offered to the listeners, enticing them to consider several possibilities in the silence before the storyteller leads them forwards.

Varying intonation patterns during the telling of a tale and use of the voice's range and strength can enliven and carry a story. A monotone delivery is to be avoided at all costs. The teller's voice needs to work alongside the meaning to conjure images in the mind of the listener, to draw the audience in and to evoke response. An expressive voice that explores its range, tone and volume will quickly bring a tale to life. Different voices for particular characters can highlight their personality traits. Whispered asides, sharp intakes of breath and unexpected changes in volume give emphasis and provide a spirited and enticing telling. Tales only come fully to life as songs, sung by a storyteller who is sensitive to the story structure, meaning and style. Highly exaggerated interpretations, however, can interfere with the spirit of the story. A fine line needs to be drawn here. Accents are probably best avoided unless they can be sustained, or only used in dialogue. Many tales include dialect words, which add authenticity and may be understood from the context.

Creative voice play builds atmosphere through word emphasis, moans, rasps, almost inaudible sighs and so on. Adding repetitive vocal noises attached to certain characters can create stronger images of creatures such as the Great Sea Bird and the Little Rainbow Fish (see *How the Tides came to Ebb and Flow*, pages 5–7). The rhythm of the squawking bird – *'squawk, squaw, squaw, squaw, squawk!'* – added by the storyteller could also be enhanced by body percussion or ritualised flapping movements. Such additions prompt the audience to join in, and foster an active engagement in the tale, which is particularly appropriate for very young audiences. These vocal effects act as mnemonic devices and encourage communal voice play each time the character appears. However, such noises are not prerequisites but merely options which can be employed to enhance particular tales.

Gestures and body movements play a significant role in supporting children's understanding of the story and in creating a sense of shared community. There is no need for a full-length mimed performance; just a few marked movements and slight gestures can extend the images conveyed or highlight emotive aspects. Physically crouching, or standing tall and proud can denote meaning and add insight. Simple head and hand movements also prompt clearer pictures of the characters, their feelings, concerns and demeanours. Repetitive refrains are often helped by accompanying gestures which focus attention and encourage the audience to join in with the actions as well as the words. In addition, a single, deliberate gesture in a moment of suspense and silence can provide the audience with a communal sense of knowing before the language of the story catches up with them.

For example, in *The Final Victory* (see pages 95–6), after Tuk has hacked his way out of the igloo, the teller could take a sharp intake of breath, move her hand to her mouth and give a sustained look of consternation. The audience will hear the noise, read the gesture and the facial expression, consider all the possibilities and select their chosen hypothesis before hearing the words spoken by the storyteller: 'There before him lay Nahnuk's lifeless body. His shelter had been blown away by the wind, and he had frozen to death...'

Facial expressions of all kinds unite the storyteller with her audience and help to convey the unspoken subtexts and the layers of meaning within the tale. These expressions change quite naturally as the story unfolds and the teller lives through it. Eye contact is a frequent feature of performance which can create a common bond, an intimacy and empathy between the teller and the told. If the audience is within her immediate field of vision, the teller can engage with them by working to connect with each listener, naturally tuning in and out of this contact at various points in the tale.

For example, in *The Children of Wax* (see pages 56–7) when Ngwabi dies in the sunlight, the teller's eyes may not at that point be offering contact but be staring down at the imagined pool of molten wax on the ground. Variety may be the key in relation to facial expression, but much of this will emerge naturally in the storytelling.

Using visual aids and artefacts is an option open to storytellers. Although tale telling does not rely upon additional stimuli, it can be contextualised and enhanced through the use of such aids. In Southern Asia, the Far East and other parts of the world, professional storytellers use artefacts such as story cloths, story dolls, boxes, scrolls, shadow puppets and masks to introduce and structure tales. Single pieces of costume and low lighting or candlelight can create atmosphere and give significance to a performance, and a sense of presence to the performer. Even the simple effect of a colourful shawl or blanket draped over the storyteller's chair gives status to the telling and signals to the children to gather round. However, these elements are not necessities and can distract from the story and the social nature of the telling if they are over-used. Much will depend on the style of telling and the tale. Visual aids can be particularly helpful for second language learners who rely heavily on visual clues to aid understanding. Objects related to the tale, such as models, slides, pictures, felt and magnet boards, can all help fill in the gaps that unknown words and phrases leave, and with young audiences single relevant artefacts can provoke interest and enrich the pictures painted by the words.

Using music and rhythm to create atmosphere and enrich a tale is another optional feature of performance. Music can sensitively interpret a story's changing moods and in many cultures is an indispensable part of storytelling. Folk and percussion instruments are frequently employed by professional storytellers to set the scene, link sections of a tale, mark significant moments and round off the telling. A talented musician can capitalise upon the opportunities that the refrains and chants of some traditional tales offer for voice and instrumental work. Some anthologies even provide music for the included tales (see Appendix 1, pages 165–79). It is possible, however, simply to chant the song to an overt rhythm, or repeat the refrain in a heavy whisper, avoiding the need to sing it alone and inviting the audience to join in.

For example, the Kookaburra's call 'Gou gour gah ghah' in *How The Sun Came Into The World* (see pages 144–5), could be repeated and turned into a song with a distinct melody line and accompanying percussion, or even sung as a round. Alternatively, it could just be whispered with a gradual crescendo, 'Gou gour gah ghah, Gou gour gah ghah, Gou gour gah ghah!' and gain a different effect.

A few guitar chords, rhythmic drumming, plaintiff notes upon a flute, or experimental use of other percussion can simply but effectively highlight the rhythmical quality of the language or the persistent beat in a refrain. Exploring aspects of body percussion such as finger clicking, hand rubbing, finger drumming and foot stamping can also create rhythmic sounds and patterns of differential volume which add pathos, interest and texture to a tale. At a simple level, by merely adding initially slow, then faster, rhythmic finger drums to mark the syllabic beat in the words 'Gou gour gah ghah, Gou gour gah ghah, Gou gour gah ghah!', the tale teller is enhancing the tune of the tale. This use of music and rhythm can be employed by storytellers whether or not they are musicians, for all teachers have a sense of rhythm which if creatively deployed can make a significant contribution to the impact of many a tale.

Elements of music and rhythm permeate many traditional tales and it is up to the teller to develop her own interplay of rhythm, pace, pitch, texture and intonation in both words and sounds. Storytellers need to become confident enough to experiment with all the various strategies which can enhance tale telling and identify those elements which can come to inhabit the very fabric of the tale.

INVOLVING THE AUDIENCE

It is the conviction and commitment of the storyteller to the spirit of the tale which really engages the audience, offering pleasure and satisfaction to both teller and listener. On many occasions the audience will remain seated. Some listeners may choose to close their eyes, while others will watch intently. Many will look but not see the teller; rather the tale itself will unfold in their imagination before them. Powerful stories weave their own webs, uniting the teller and told and creating a rapport which is at once both individual and social, for storytelling is an interactive and shared experience. Sometimes the listeners will take a more physically or vocally active part, but the way in which they become involved will depend on the tale, the style of telling and the audience themselves.

It may be helpful to inform children about the nature of the story to be shared, explaining, for example, that *The Weaving of a Dream* (see pages 161–4) is a tale to listen to silently, or that *How the Crab got its Back* (see pages 128–9) has a repetitive refrain with which they can join in.

Whatever the expectation of audience participation, the quality of listening will be enhanced through the shared experience of journeying into a story. Personal connections speak volumes; even sharing the reasons for the choice of tale can provide links, set the frame and interest the listeners.

Direct reference to the audience can prompt further involvement, as in the tale of *The Weaving of a Dream* where descriptions of the beautiful brocade and the fairy palace provide scope for the teller to ask 'Can you picture it? Would you like to live there?' Rhetorical, ritual or genuine questions can be added to many tales to invite response or provoke imaginative engagement.

Asides to the audience are also effective tools for developing the intimate social bond of telling. For example, as an aside in *The End of Baba Yaga* (see pages 31–2) the storyteller could comment about Vasseila that 'she was like another young and beautiful heroine that I can recall'. This metanarrative comment referring to Cinderella serves to unite the teller and told in their common knowledge, as they stand momentarily alongside the story. Similar touches in a tale can create a corporate conspiracy of knowing – for example, 'What I know and what you know, but what Baba Yaga didn't know was that there was a human hiding in her house!' – and offer a space for communal reflection upon the tale.

Tuning into the audience is essential for the storyteller, not only in the selection of an appropriate tale but in the moment-to-moment exchange of the story as it unfolds. The response of the audience, shown in almost imperceptible movements, eye contact and facial expressions, provides the teller with critical information which can redirect the tale in subtle ways, shift the orientation of characters or develop particular features. Storytelling is a collaborative enterprise, a social process, so tales are constantly renewed and refreshed in each retelling in interaction with each audience.

At the close of a tale, silence often reigns. This experience is a feature of the oral tradition and is worth savouring and sustaining. When questions, comments and queries do emerge, these need to be pondered upon and discussed by all the audience, not just responded to by the storyteller, since once the tale has been told, it is owned by everyone and is therefore common property to investigate, examine and retell.

Learning to tell stories in the classroom is very worthwhile, and extremely satisfying. After the tale has been selected, its shape committed to memory, and practised, it is ready to be played into existence in interaction with the audience. The voice is used in an instrumental and creative manner alongside gesture, pace, music, and/or artefacts to share the flavour and spirit of the tale. This combination of commitment to the tale, a playful attitude and personal conviction in the truth of the story lies at the heart of storytelling.

THE WEAVING OF A DREAM
A Chinese tale

Once, in a land far to the East, there lived a widow and her three sons, Leme, Letuie and Leje. They lived a simple life together: the young men chopped wood to sell and the old widow spent her days weaving brocades. She had a special gift for this and was well known for miles around for the beautiful brocades and tapestries she wove. In her fingers these almost seemed to come alive with fruit, flowers, birds and animals.

One day, while she was at the market selling her work, she happened upon a stall displaying paintings. One of these, far more arresting than the others, caught her eye. It was of a palace, overflowing with flowers and birds; fish swam in the river that ran through its gardens and a brilliant sun warmed the painting and its occupants with a glowing hue. Everything the old woman had ever dreamed about seemed encapsulated here before her. Her heart was filled with joy as she examined every detail of this representation of her dreams. Unable to stop herself, she traded all her brocades for the painting and instead of returning home with rice for her sons she returned home with this painting of her desires and dreams. Three times she paused on her journey home to unroll the scroll and gaze at it in wonder. 'If only I could live there,' she whispered to herself.

At home Leme and Letuie were impatient with her: 'What good is this to us?' they demanded. 'We cannot eat it.'

Only her youngest son, Leje, understood her deep desire to dwell in this palace of paradise, to inhabit her perfect dream.

'Mother,' he suggested, 'why don't you do a weaving of the painting? Your brocades are so lifelike it would almost be like living there.'

'Yes, my son,' she replied, 'you are right. That is the nearest I will ever come to living there. I must do this or die of sorrow and loss.'

She set to work that very night, and once she started she simply didn't stop. As days passed into weeks and weeks into months, the widow worked on and on. Leme and Letuie chided their mother, telling her that they were tired of earning all the money. They even tried to prevent her physically from weaving her palace of paradise, but Leje intervened. 'Let mother be or else she will die of grief. I will chop the wood for us all,' he said.

So the old widow continued to weave, never stopping, working all day and well into the night, when she had to work by candlelight. The smoke burned into her eyes and made them red and sore. After one year, when tears caused by the candlelight fell, she wove them into the fish pond and flowing river. After two years, when her worn fingers spent drops of blood upon the shuttle, she wove these into the glowing sun and scarlet flowers. After three years she finished it. It was the most beautiful brocade ever seen. The palace was woven in rich hues and threads, its glorious gardens strewn with flowers. The tiny songbirds seemed to sing from the surface; the fish swam, the river sparkled and the red sun warmed every silken thread.

The widow rubbed her eyes, and a smile spread slowly across her lined and tired face. Her sons stood admiring her work, and then suddenly a great wind blew the door of their hut open. It raced into the room, released the brocade from the loom and whisked it out of the open window and up into the sky. They rushed outside, calling and shouting, but it was gone. It had vanished. Returning to the hut, the sons found their mother on the doorstep, pale and unconscious. When she came round, she pleaded with her eldest son to go East, to follow the wind and find her brocade.

'It means more to me than my own life,' she told him earnestly.

Leme set out straightaway, and a month later he came to the top of a mountain on which there was perched a strange house made of stone, with a stone horse standing by the door. An old crone, who was sitting outside her home, enquired where he was heading.

'I'm going East,' said Leme, 'to where the wind has carried off a beautiful brocade my mother has spent three years weaving.'

'Ah that,' nodded the fortune-teller. 'The fairies of Sun Mountain sent the wind to bring it to them. They wish to copy its beautiful design. It certainly is a difficult and dangerous journey.'

'How do I get there?' demanded Leme.

'First, young man, you must knock out your two front teeth and place them in the mouth of my stone horse. He will then be able to move and eat the ten red berries growing on my bush. He will carry you to Sun Mountain, but on the way you must pass over Flame Mountain which is constantly on fire. I warn you that you must not call out, even if the pain is unbearable, for if you do you will be burned to ashes. Next you will come to the Sea of Ice – again, you must not make a sound, although it will be bitterly cold, or else your body will be dashed to the bottom of the sea. If you pass through these places you will reach Sun Mountain, where you may be given your mother's brocade.'

Leme shivered. He felt both hot and cold with fear. His face grew pale; he shook his head. The fortune-teller cackled, 'Young man, it seems you could not endure it, and after all you need not. Take this box of gold with you and go home to your mother.'

Leme, pleased at this turn of events, hurried away from the fortune-teller with the gold, and realising how much more he would have if he kept it to himself, he took a different path at the foot of the mountain and headed towards the big city.

Back at home, Letuie and Leje waited with their mother, who was growing weaker by the day. When two months had passed and no word from Leme had come, she asked Letuie to go East and find her brocade.

'It means more to me than my own life,' she told him desperately.

So Letuie also set out, and soon found himself talking to the crone at the door of the stone house. He listened to her tale of the fire and ice, and how he must knock out his two front teeth, and he too shivered and shook his head. So he was sent home with a box of gold, but being a greedy youth he went instead to the big city to spend this fortune on himself.

The old widow waited, hoping daily for her sons' return with her precious brocade. Finally, Leje could stand it no longer. He persuaded his mother that he would go East and find both the life-giving brocade and his two brothers who must surely be injured. In half the time it had taken his brothers, Leje found his way to the fortune-teller's house. She repeated the instructions and he stood firm before her, refusing her offer of gold. 'I must fetch my mother's brocade or she will surely die,' he told her and, picking up a stone, he knocked out his two front teeth and fed them to the stone horse. After the horse had eaten the ten berries, Leje jumped on to its back and clung on tightly as the amazing creature leaped high into the sky. It chased after the wind for three days and three nights until they reached Flame Mountain. The heat was unbearable. The stone horse plunged through the fire and Leje felt flames biting through his flesh, but he clenched his teeth, closed his eyes and did not cry out.

In half a day's time, they came out of the flames and stood on the shores of the Sea of Ice. Leje spurred his horse onwards and steam began to rise from his body as the ice-cold water stung against his skin. He felt a bitter numbness descend, but he uttered no sound at all.

In half a day's time he came through the Sea of Ice, and there before him stood Sun Mountain. The strength of the sun comforted him and began to ease the pain and heal his wounds.

The fairies' palace was nestled inside the sun, or so it seemed, and drifting from the open windows he could hear the sounds of women singing, talking and laughing. Down from his horse he jumped, and without fear Leje opened the door to the palace and strode inside. He found himself in a great hall filled with fairies, all weaving as fast as they could and copying his mother's brocade which hung in the very centre of the room. At the sight of this mortal the fairies froze, their eyes showing their panic. Leje explained his mission and his mother's dreams and desires, and gradually their fear subsided. They asked him to stay with them for one night so he could regain his strength, as this would allow them a final night of weaving to finish their work. Leje agreed. He ate the food prepared for him and fell into a deep and healing sleep.

The fairies did not sleep, however. When the sun set, a fairy hung up a shining pearl to fill the room with light so that they could continue weaving.

Later, the finest fairy weaver, on finishing her section, was disappointed when she found that compared to the widow's brocade her own was poor. 'The original brocade is so perfect, a real palace of paradise,' thought the fairy, and so she began to weave herself into the old widow's brocade as a tiny red fairy dancing in a ray of sunshine.

At the first light of day, the exhausted fairies slept on, but Leje awoke, took down his mother's brocade and ran to his waiting horse. Three days and three nights later, he stood before the fortune-teller's house. She congratulated him and, taking his teeth from the stone horse's mouth, she placed them back in Leje's mouth. It was as if they had never gone. 'Quickly, you must return home,' she told him, 'for your mother is dying of grief and is as weak as a single thread of silk. Wear these embroidered boots. They will speed you on your way.'

In almost an instant, Leje was at his mother's side. He spread the brocade over her feeble form and the warmth of its sun began to draw her back into life. The old woman gazed at this tapestried dream of her hopes and desires and saw with surprise the tiny red fairy. Her thin fingers touched the woven fairy and in that instant a gentle breeze danced in through the window. It seemed that as it blew, the brocade grew larger and larger, longer and wider until its silken threads covered everything in sight. The old hut disappeared and before their very eyes the brocade began to come to life. The palace, the gardens, the songbirds, the sun and even the red fairy all became real to the touch.

So it was that her dream was woven into being through the love one son bore for his mother. It is said that Leje married the red fairy, and that Leme and Letuie returned when they heard people talk of their mother's fortunes. But I believe that when they saw her happiness and thought of their desertion they crept away shamefaced, for they had taken no part in the weaving of her dream. I wonder, did you?

A SELECTION OF
TRADITIONAL-TALE TEXTS

A multiplicity of traditional-tale texts exist and are added to continuously by publishers aware of the power and potency of such books at home and at school. Some tales operate as a 'script' for the storyteller, enabling her to bring the tale to life through word of mouth. Others through considerable literary reshaping have become perhaps somewhat less accessible for the novice storyteller to retell. All, however, represent possible source material for oral storytelling, although individuals will make their own choices and will seek out tales which they like and which will work for them.

This appendix offers a range of books and audio cassettes which can be used in the classroom. An approximate age has been noted beside the title of each annotated tale. These refer to children reading them, not to hearing them told, and are only a guide. The overall selection can only reflect a small proportion of the rich diversity of tales currently available from across the world. It is offered, however, as a point of reference for establishing 'Traditional-tale book boxes' in schools and extending the variety of such texts which are readily available in classrooms.

Despite the excellence of many of these texts and audio cassettes, there is no substitute for being part of a live oral story performance. To achieve this, teachers and children need the opportunity to develop their own storytelling skills and to work alongside professional oral storytellers in the school context. Personal recommendations are worth pursuing, but in addition the Society for Storytelling publishes a *Directory of Storytellers* which is available from SfS Education, PO Box 2344, Reading RG6 7FG.

The annotated tales are organised into sections which highlight their country of origin and include folk tales, myths, legends and fairy tales, both traditional and modern. A trend in recent years has been to parody and experiment with popular traditional tales, and examples of these are also included. ('PB' after the publisher and age range indicates a picture-book edition.)

TRADITIONAL TALES FROM AROUND THE WORLD

COLLECTIONS OF TALES FROM AROUND THE WORLD

Folk Tales and Fables of the World
edited by Barbara Hayes, illustrated by Robert Ingpen
(Dragons World) age 10+
This large book contains many favourite tales including *The Pedlar of Swaffham*, *Aladdin*, *Baba Yaga*, *David and Goliath* and *Johnny Appleseed*, as well as some less well-known tales. The aboriginal stories and the tales from Asia are particularly evocative.

Time for Telling
selected by Mary Medlicott, illustrated by Sue Williams
(Kingfisher) age 7+
A delightful collection of tales from the oral tradition recorded by storytellers from around the globe. There is much here to encourage the novice storyteller and facilitate active participation.

The Singing Sack: 28 Stories from Around the World
compiled by Helen East, illustrated by Mary Currie
(A & C Black) teacher resource
An unusual anthology, with music, stories, songs, a cassette (with songs in different languages) and detailed background notes. An extremely valuable, flexible and interesting resource for storytelling.

A Web of Stories
by Grace Hallworth
(Mammoth) age 9+
An inviting title, with spider tales from Greece, Ghana, Australia, Mexico and India. The collection illuminates how spiders have become woven into the folklore, wisdom and cultural practices of many communities.

Clever Gretchen and Other Forgotten Folktales
retold by Alison Lurie, illustrated by Margot Tomes
(Mammoth) age 9+
An enjoyable collection of some less well-known tales which feature strong, intelligent, resourceful and beautiful heroines; an antidote to the more helpless and hapless heroines existing elsewhere.

Mythical Mazes, A Collection of Amazing Mythical Mazes
retold by Dugald Steer
(Templar) age 9+
An innovative text which reconstructs the epic journeys of heroes
from myths and legends as a visual story maze as well as a tale to tell.
The reader is invited, for example, to quest alongside Sir Gawain as
he searches for the Green Knight, and then to read the story.

Two Tongue Tale (resource pack and two tapes)
produced by The National Community Teachers' Resource
available from The Children's Book Foundation, London
The tapes feature little known folk tales in Bengali, Urdu, Yoruba,
Turkish, Gujarati, Arabic and English with translations and
accompanying call and response openers. The pack includes a poster,
traditional music, maps and background information. The interviews
with storytellers from different countries provide fascinating
information and make this a valuable resource.

THE BRITISH ISLES

Book of British Fairy Tales
Alan Garner, illustrated by Derek Collard
(Collins) age 9+
This collection evocatively re-creates the rhythmic and vernacular
voice of the oral storyteller on the page. Some are familiar like *Kate
Crackernuts* and *Molly Whuppy*; others are less well known.

The British Isles Book of British Fairytales
English Fairy Tales, collected by Margery Gill
(Bodley Head) age 10+
A good source book which contains both Jacobs' original volumes,
English Fairytales and *More English Fairy Tales*, as well as Jacobs'
notes and references. An interesting collection for comparison with
the many picture-book retellings of tales such as *Lazy Jack, Henry
Penny, Teeny Tiny* and *Jack and the Beanstalk*.

Jack and the Beanstalk
Alan Garner, illustrated by Julek Heller
(Collins) age 4+ PB
The oral roots of the tale are self-evident in this powerful retelling,
which is dramatically illustrated. An enduring tale of foolishness,
mystery, fear and perseverance.

Sir Gawain and the Loathly Lady
retold by Selina Hastings, illustrated by Juan Wijngaard
(Walker Books) age 9+ PB
The Arthurian legends come to life here through the rich literary prose and the detailed and exquisite illustrations.

The Broonies, Silkies and Fairies
Traveller tales by Duncan Williamson, illustrated by Alan Herriot
(Cannongate) age 9+
These tales share the sorrows and dangers which many country folk endured, and explore the threads of the supernatural which were woven into their living and the landscape. The informative introduction and the accompanying information is personal and engaging.

The Selkie Girl
retold by Susan Cooper, illustrated by Warwick Hutton
(Aladdin) age 8+ PB
A lyrical and haunting retelling of this well-travelled tale about the selkie girl whose skin the Scotsman steals to secure her presence.

Tales for the Telling, Irish Folk and Fairy Stories
by Edna O'Brien, illustrated by Michael Foreman
(Puffin) age 7+
A diverse collection of tales of Irish people, the little people and the giants; rich folk and poor folk, wise and foolish all find a home here. No notes support the tales but many would bear retelling.

THE REST OF EUROPE

The Fat Cat: A Danish Folktale
translated and illustrated by Jack Kent
(Picture Puffin) age 5+ PB
A delightful cumulative tale reminiscent of 'There was an old woman who swallowed a fly'. The cat eats each character he meets, getting fatter and fatter, until he meets a woodcutter...

East of the Sun and West o' the Moon: A Norwegian Fairytale
retold by Naomi Lewis, illustrated by P.J. Lynch
(Walker Books) age 8+ PB
This epic encompasses almost all possible components of fairy tales: rags and riches, magic and mystery, a curse, a quest, romance and passion, and even a happy ending.

PRIMARY
PROFESSIONAL BOOKSHELF

The Orchard Book of Greek Myths
retold by Geraldine McCaughrean, illustrated by Emma Chichester Clark
(Orchard) age 7+
A handsomely produced book which make the Greek myths both accessible and attractive. There are no accompanying notes but the tales are tempting and reap their own rewards.

AFRICA

Bury my Bones, but Keep my Words: African Tales for Telling
retold by Tony Fairman, illustrated by Meshack Asare
(Collins) age 7+
A wonderful book which creates a real sense of Africa. The tales are full of life, and demand audience involvement with repetitive refrains, chants and songs, and memorable language and imagery. Lots of support for the novice storyteller.

The River that Went to the Sky: Twelve Tales by African Storytellers
ed. Mary Medlicott, illustrated by Ademola Akintola
(Kingfisher) age 8+
All twelve of these traditional and contemporary tales are superbly retold by professional storytellers and story writers. The story and author's notes provide insight and authenticity and highlight the way personal stories persistently inhabit folklore retellings. These stories deserve a wide audience, although not all lend themselves to oral storytelling.

Chinye: A West African Folktale
by Obi Onyefulu, illustrated by Erie Safarewicz
(Frances Lincoln) age 6+ PB
This text captures the African tradition of storytelling and tells of how young Chinye is forced into the night to collect water. The forest spirits protect her but are not quite so generous with her spoilt stepsister who disobeys their instructions. The tale lends itself to retelling and dramatic exploration.

Oh Kojo! How Could You!
by Verna A Ardema, illustrated by Marc Brown
(Picturemac) age 5+ PB
Oh Kojo! How Could You is an amusing Anancy story which shares a plot with *Jack and the Beanstalk* and is illustrated in a lively fashion.

THE AMERICAN HERITAGE FROM AFRICA

Listen to this Story: Tales from the West Indies
retold by Grace Hallworth
(Magnet) age 6+
Cric Crac. A Collection of West Indian Stories
retold by Grace Hallworth
(Mammoth) age 6+
These two texts are written in an accessible and colourful style. They demand to be told, and encourage joining in with noises, singsong phrases and actions. Brer Anancy, the trickster, is the central character in many of these supernatural tales of magic, mystery and mischief.

NORTH AND SOUTH AMERICAN TALES

The Faber Book of North American Legends
ed. Virginia Haviland, illustrated by Ann Strugnett
(Faber) age 10+
This collection comprises stories from the American Indians and Eskimos, Black Americans, European immigrants, and indigenous American 'tall tales'. The reader can meet an Indian Cinderella and the Tar Baby as well as The Twist Mouth Family and Pecos Bill. A valuable anthology reflecting a rich heritage of folklore.

Native North American Stories
retold by Robert Hull, illustrated by Richard Hook and Claire Robinson (Teacher resource)
(Wayland) age 8+
This superb collection offers so much more than the tales themselves, which are rhythmic, direct and conveyed with condensed power. There are also introductions to each of the tales and detailed notes on the creatures, culture and country which the North Americans inhabited.

Central and South American Stories
retold by Robert Hull, illustrated by Vanessa Cleall and Claire Robinson
(Wayland) age 8+
Another in the excellent Wayland series, with notes, designs and motifs from South American art and introductions to each tale. The colour illustrations are also strong. The stories themselves are consistently well told; a real resource for storytelling.

How Night Came
by Joanna Troughton
(Blackie) age 5+ PB
This creation myth from the Tupi Indians of the Amazon explains how night was released from captivity beneath the waters. The illustrations are strong, and the language lively; good for retelling.

RUSSIA

Old Peter's Russian Tales
retold by Arthur Ransome, illustrated by Faith Jaques
(Cape) age 7+
The classic folk tales in this book are powerful and resonant, and demand to be re-read and retold. Ransome links the tales together through conversations between a grandfather and his grandchildren, creating a still satisfying whole, some 80 plus years after it was first published in 1916.

Baba Yaga
retold and illustrated by Katya Arnold
(North South) age 6+ PB
An intriguingly illustrated tale of the legendary Baba Yaga who flies in her pestle and mortar across the skies. At last a picture-book retelling of this dramatic character from Russian folklore; useful material for a book box or classroom shelf.

Ukrainian Folk Tales
by Christina Oparenko
(Oxford University Press) age 9+
These lively tales are told with a distinctly oral flavour which supports retelling. Brief notes and occasional recipes for Ukrainian dishes mentioned in the tales contribute to make this an unusual and interesting text.

AUSTRALIA

What Made Tiddalik Laugh
by Joanna Troughton
(Blackie) age 5+
A delightful dream-time tale about a giant frog who drinks all the water in the world. Wonderful material for participation storytelling in the early years, and for reworking in other contexts or with a more contemporary perspective.

ASIA

Seasons of Splendour: Tales, Myths and Legends of India
by Madhur Jaffrey, illustrated by Michael Foreman
(Puffin) age 8+
A rich collection of short stories. Each tale provides a sense of insight into Madhur Jaffrey's childhood and the Hindu calendar. The style is conversational and draws from the oral tradition. Punctuation notes are provided, and the tales lend themselves to telling or reading aloud.

The White Crane
illustrated by Junko Morimot
(Collins) age 7+ PB
A stunning and evocative retelling of this classic Japanese folk tale about giving and receiving love, and keeping promises. This tale, with its powerful illustrations, is a story to tell and tell again. *The Shoemaker and the Elves* has a similar plot but a happier ending.

The Willow Pattern Story
retold by Allan Drummond
(North-South Books) age 8+ PB
This is one of the many tales told to explain the design on 'blue willow' pattern china. This sensitive and poetic retelling has informative background details and quality illustrations.

The Seven Chinese Brothers
by Margaret Mahy, illustrated by Jean and Mou-sen Tseng
(Pan Macmillan) age 8+ PB
This ancient folk tale dates from the time of Emperor Ch'in Shih Huang, who planned the construction of the Great Wall of China. The beautifully illustrated tale tells of how the seven brothers intervene to reduce the suffering of the workers building the Wall. The text leans on the oral tradition and has a clear structure with plenty of repetition and narrator asides.

Grandfather Tang's Story
by Ann Tompert, illustrated by Robert Andrew Parker
(Julia MacRae) age 6+ PB
This traditional Chinese tale is cleverly retold by Grandfather Tang who uses tangrams to reconstruct the story of the fox fairies for Little Soo. The ancient Chinese puzzles are innovatively and effectively used.

The Korean Cinderella
by Shirley Climo, illustrated by Ruth Heller
(HarperCollins) age 7+ PB
This fabulously illustrated retelling emerged from three Korean variations of the Cinderella story. The heroine, Pear Blossom, nicknamed Little Pig by her stepmother, is worked relentlessly, but assisted by a frog, some sparrows and a black ox she finds her prince.

TRADITIONAL FAIRY TALES, FABLES AND LITERARY TALES

The Faber Book of Favourite Fairy Tales
by Ed Sara and Stephen Corrin, illustrated by Juan Wijngaard
(Faber) age 7+
A stunning volume in which the reader can revisit many well-known fairy tales from Grimm, Andersen, Perrault and Jacobs.

The Brothers Grimm: Popular Folk Tales
by Brian Alderson, illustrated by Michael Foreman
(Gollancz) age 7+
This splendid collection is written remembering the oral tradition, richly complemented by Foreman's illustrations.

The Twelve Dancing Princesses
illustrated by Errol Le Cain
(Puffin) age 5+ PB
This visual interpretation fits the classical fairy-tale mould with beautiful princesses, a sumptuous castle and noble lords, all in stark contrast to the poverty stricken soldier in his invisible cloak.

The Flying Trunk and Other Stories from Andersen
retold by Naomi Lewis, illustrated by various artists
(Beaver) age 7+
This varied collection is illustrated by well-known children's artists, including Tony Ross, Ruth Brown, and David McKee.

Thumbelina
retold by James Riordan, illustrated by Wayne Andersen
(Red Fox) age 8+ PB
An imaginative and haunting retelling of this popular Hans Andersen tale. The illustrations are enchanting, magical and memorable.

Hans Andersen: His Classic Fairy Tales
Translated byErik Hugard, illustrated by Michael Foreman
(Gollancz) age 7+
This superb translation is a selection of 18 of Andersen's literary fairy tales. Foreman's illustrations enhance the stories which are favourites with children.

The Little Match Girl
by Hans Christian Andersen, illustrated by Rachel Isadora
(Picture Knight) age 7+ PB
The Victorian street illustrations complement this poignant tale and bring the tale's messages to the forefront. The layout and structure of the text lends itself to retelling through the pictures.

Stories for Children
by Oscar Wilde, illustrated by P.J. Lynch
(Simon & Schuster) age 7+
A superlative edition which retains all the strength of the original writing but also offers marvellous illustrations of a magical nature. A quality text to be treasured, owned and shared.

Aesop's Fables
by Lisbeth Zwerger
(Picture Book Studio) age 7+
The gentle ink and wash illustrations which face each short fable soften the imperative of the separately stated moral.

The Selfish Giant
by Oscar Wilde, illustrated by S. Saelig Gallagher
(Macdonald Young Books) age 6+ PB
This remarkable representation of the well-known tale is both powerful and haunting. The significant themes are raised and reflected upon in the evocative illustrations. A must for the classroom bookshelf.

Fairy Tales
by Terry Jones, illustrated by Michael Foreman
(Puffin) age 7+
An acclaimed collection of modern fairy tales cooked from traditional recipes. The brevity, accessible language and strong structures of the tales make them particularly suitable for retelling, and very popular with children of all ages.

ALTERNATIVE RETELLINGS OF TRADITIONAL TALES

The Practical Princess and Other Liberating Fairy Tales
by Jay Williams, illustrations by Rick Schreiter
(Hippo) age 7+
This collection of modern feminist folk tales is refreshing, and makes genuinely amusing reading. Meet Sir Philbert Fitzhugh the fearful, and the extremely practical Princess Bedelia.

There's a Wolf in my Pudding: Twelve Twisted, Tortured, Grim and Gruesome, Tall and Terrible Tales
by David Henry Wilson, illustrated by Jonathon Allen
(Piper) age 7+
A selection of traditional tales are hilariously retold here, either from the perspective of one of the characters or as an alternative version. A popular collection for retelling which encourages the adoption of alternative angles and storyteller asides.

The Fwog Prince: The Twuth
by Kaye Umansky
(Puffin) age 8+
A humorous retelling of this fairy tale which attempts to explain 'the whole twuth, and nothing but the twuth', about the original tale. A sustained romp with Proud Prince Pipsqueak and Princess Petulant.

Ten in a Bed
by Allan Ahlberg, illustrated by Andre Amstutz
(Puffin) age 8+
This delightful parody of fairy tales weaves in a plethora of characters who meet Dinah Price, the heroine, and journey with her through the many layers of tales in the book. Another Ahlberg treat which plays on the reader's knowledge of the genre.

The Stinky Cheese Man and other Fairly Stupid Tales
by Jon Scieszka and Lane Smith
(Puffin) age 8+
An anarchic trip through the world of traditional tales, with suitably surreal illustrations and innovative typography. This is rich material for group reading and discussion of text conventions as well as a model for changing stories and experimenting with the genre.

Hairy Tales and Nursery Crimes
by Michael Rosen, illustrated by Alan Baker
(Young Lions Series) age 7+
In this collection of tales, Rosen masterfully experiments with words, sounds, stories and meanings. This original work alters key elements in tales and explores the consequences with heaps of humour and satire.

Trail of Stones
by Gwen Strauss, illustrated by Anthony Browne
(Julia MacRae) age 10+
A haunting collection of poems about various fairy-tale characters. Their personal perspectives are powerfully expressed and expose surprising emotions and revealing attitudes.

The Three Little Wolves and the Big Bad Pig
by Eugene Trivizas, illustrated by Helen Oxenbury
(Mammoth) age 7+ PB
A hilarious read which involves the three little wolves in building stronger and stronger houses as the Big Bad Pig, with less puff and more modern equipment, attempts to capture them.

The True Story of the Three Little Pigs By a Wolf
as told to Jon Scieszka, illustrated by Lane Smith
(Viking Kestrel) age 7+ PB
The tale is retold from the Wolf's point of view, and is full of humour and wonderfully illustrated. It lends itself to retelling as well.

The Frog Prince continued
by Jon Scieszka, paintings by Lane Smith
(Viking) age 8+ PB
In this follow-up to the classic tale of the frog prince, the princess and her new husband are not living in wedded bliss. The prince decides he wants to be turned back into a frog and journeys into the woods and the world of fairy tales to find a witch capable of such a feat.

The Book that Jack Wrote
by Jon Scieszka, paintings by Daniel Adel
(Viking) age 5+ PB
A successful and rhythmic retelling of *This is the House that Jack Built* which integrates nursery rhymes and children's stories into a surprising and satisfying whole. The bold illustrations are intriguing.

Snow White in New York
by Fiona French
(Oxford University Press) age 7+ PB
Set in the film era of the 1950s, Snow White is taken to downtown New York to be shot, but survives through singing solo for the seven jazzmen. Later, however, a poisoned cocktail finds its way into her hands. A popular retelling for all ages.

Somebody and the Three Blairs
by Marilyn Tolhurst, illustrated by Simone Abel
(Softbacks) age 5+ PB
This engagingly illustrated book is set in the modern household of Mr Blair, Mrs Blair and Baby Blair. 'Somebody' is a big teddy. The play on words and partial extension of the 'original' tale here adds much to the pleasure of this text. This is a tale for children to revisit and re-read together.

Hansel and Gretel
The Brothers Grimm, illustrated by Anthony Browne
(Little Mammoth) age 8+ PB
A remarkable text which places the tale in a bleak and deprived contemporary home. The parallels are drawn in carefully: the witch's broom next to the ironing board, the window panes as bars. The gripping and fearful illustrations take the reader expertly through the dramatic tale to the eventual release and reconciliation.

Rumplestiltskin
retold and illustrated by Paul O Zelinsky
(Aurum Press) age 7+ PB
An intriguing retelling of this Grimm tale which provides an alternative perspective upon the tale as it focuses on the relationship between the miller's daughter/queen and her husband, the king. An interesting angle, well developed, which weaves other threads about this tale.

Jim and the Beanstalk
by Raymond Briggs
(Puffin) age 7+ PB
This enjoyable retelling by Raymond Briggs involves Jim playing the good Samaritan to a bald, toothless, short-sighted giant he meets at the top of the beanstalk. However, the giant's appetite for 'fried boy' sandwiches returns...

Stone Soup
by Tony Ross
(Beaver) age 4+ PB
A witty retelling of this classic folk tale. The illustrations delight and engage as the Wolf undertakes endless household chores for wise Mother Hen while she calmly cooks his soup.

AUDIO CASSETTES OF TRADITIONAL TALES

A brief but significant guide to traditional tales on audio cassette is offered here; some are read, many are told. Such tapes offer regional voices and dialects and represent a real resource in the classroom. Professional storytellers often produce their own tapes to sell and the Society for Storytelling also produces a catalogue of tales on tape, entitled *Talk Shop*, which provides an additional and valuable list.

The story of Rumplestiltskin
retold by Jonathan Langley, read by Victoria Wood
(Collins Audio) age 6 +

Fairy Tales
by Tony Ross, read by Sir Michael Hordern
(Random Century Tell a Story) age 5+

Look Lively Rest and Easy
compiled by Helen East
(A & C Black) age 6+

The Little Mermaid
by Hans Christian Andersen, read by Cathleen Nesbitt
(Collins Caedmon) age 7+

Jason and the Golden Fleece
The Travels of Ulysses
retold by Andrew Lang, read by Anthony Hyde
(Random Century Tell a Story) age 8+

Winter Tales
The Company of Storytellers
(3 Church Terrace, Alysham, Norfolk NRII 6EU) age 7+

Niamh and the Giant
Fionn MacComhail and the Dark Pool
Storyteller Vol. 1 & 2
Irish Tales
retold by Eddie Lenihan
(The Peckled Pipers) age 7+
39 Fore St., Hartland, Bideford, Devon EX39 6BE

Five Celtic Tales of Enchantment
Five Bardic Mysteries
Five Legendary Histories of Britain
retold by Robin Williamson
(The Peckled Pipers) age 10+

A Ball of Fire and Other Stories
written and read by Grace Hallworth
selected from her book *Mouth Open, Story Jump Out*
(Culture Waves Storyteller Audio Books) age 9+

The Devils Mare and Other Stories
by Evan Jones and Grace Hallworth, read by Grace Hallworth
(Culture Waves Jewels of the Caribbean Series) age 8+

Boom Chicka Boom: Stories and Rhymes to Share
by Liz Weir
(The O'Brien Press, 20 Victoria Road, Dublin 6) age 5+

Mary and the Seal People
by Duncan Williamson
(Linda Williamson, Fal Field Bank, Pete Inn, Cupar, Fife KY15 5LL)

Tales from the Vale
(The Little Cobblestone Maker and The Moors the Merrier)
by Taffy Thomas
(Northumberland Co. Library, The Willows, Morpeth NE 61 1 TA)

NOTES ON THE RETOLD TALES

HOW THE TIDES CAME TO EBB AND FLOW

I heard this tale at a school's storytelling festival in Eugene, Oregon, USA. The children joined in eagerly and I retold it in England almost immediately, their refrains still ringing in my ears. It is a satisfying story which seeks to explain much more than how the tides came to ebb and flow, and clearly uses repetitive chants, a strong structure and the number three. This traditional tale demands to be played with in performance, with repetitive actions, additional rhythmic dialogue and audience participation being central to it.

LADDER TO THE SKY

I found this dramatic legend retold in a picture book by Barbara Juster Esbensen and Helen K. Davie (Little, Brown). It is based on the Ojibway chief Kah-ge-gah-bowh's work about the customs, legends and past of his people, entitled *The Traditional History and Characteristic Sketches of the Ojibway Nation* by George Copway (a name taken by the chief), published in 1850 by Charles Gilpin in London. In their own language, the Ojibway people are known as the Anishinabe, the original people. The tale is evocatively illustrated with traditional patterns and motifs, and sensitively told using lyrical phrases, some of which are echoed in this retelling.

Pronunciation notes
Manitou – Man-ee-too
Muk-kuk – Muh-cook
Anisinhabe – Anish-in-ah-bay
Ojibway – O-jee-bway
Midi-wi-win – Midee-wee-win

THE END OF BABA YAGA

I first heard this tale at the 'Storytelling in Hope' Club run by Tony Alwyin in Eltham, South London. I have encountered many other tales about this familiar character from Russian folklore but none that so summarily finishes her off. Joan Aiken retells a similar tale entitled 'Baba Yaga's Daughter' in her collection *The Kingdom Under the Sea*

(Jonathan Cape). Baba Yaga can be both fearsome and friendly depending on her mood. She appears in hundreds of folk tales in one form or another, always flying in her mortar and pestle across the countryside and dwelling deep in the dark woods, in a strange hut that stands on a cockerel's foot.

Pronunciation notes
Vasseila – Vass-ila
Baba Yaga – Ba-ba-Ya-ga

THE CHILDREN OF WAX

I first heard this tale told at a storytelling festival in Birmingham. The teacher who shared it had developed her tale from an oral story told to her. A year later I found a written version in Alexander McCall Smith's superb collection of African folk tales entitled *Children of Wax* (Canongate). My retelling is a combination of both the oral and the written texts, influenced, no doubt, by my own children's desire to explore and investigate, and their ceaseless care for one another. McCall Smith records he collected his tales from the old people in Zimbabwe, and in particular those in Matabeleland where the range of blue granite mountains, the Matopos lie. The Ndebele people came to Matabeleland in the early nineteenth century, and it is from their oral tradition that this tale is taken. Their language is poetic, with a lyrical musical flavour to it; it is that I have tried to capture here.

Pronunciation notes
Ngwabi – Nug-waa-bee
Matopos – Mat-oh-pos

THE FINAL VICTORY

I heard Mark Cremin from Kingston University tell this tale in a classroom and followed up his reference to it in *Work in English and Drama* by Giles Bird and Jay Norris (Oxford University Press). Through countless retellings and classroom examinations of this arctic tale, I think the intense rivalry of the hunters has come to the fore, and the power of the elemental gods in contrast to the merely mortal strength of men has, I hope, surfaced.

Pronunciation notes
Tuk – Took
Nahnuk – Nah-nook

HOW THE SUN CAME INTO THE WORLD

There are many different tales from the mystical dream-time about the origin of the sun, all involving different animals. This tale is based on a retelling by Barbara Hayes in *Folktales and Fables of the World* (Appendix 1). The Aboriginals believe that long ago in the dream-time, giant creatures rose up out of the plains and that these mythical beings looked like animals, plants or insects but behaved just like humans. They believe they are directly descended from these mythical beings who bond them to every form of life in the land, both animate and inanimate. So the Emu, the Brolga (a similar but larger bird) and the Kookaburra in this tale are all ancestral beings, the spiritual totems and ancestors of different aboriginal tribes.

Pronunciation notes
Dineewan – Din-ee-wahn
Gougourghah – Goo-gour-gah
Murrumbidgee – Ma-rum-bid-gee

HOW THE CRAB GOT ITS BACK

I heard Grace Hallworth tell this tale at an 'Evening of Storytelling' and later read it in her delightful collection *Listen to This Story* (Appendix 1). All the tales in this book are recalled from her childhood in the West Indies. In my retelling I use the old woman's refrain more frequently to build the suspense, mystery and tension. Children like to join in this chorus, inviting first Esmerelda, then Yolanda to scratch their backs. As Grace records, such folk tales were part of the land and of the people of the West Indies and demand to be told and retold, reshaped and resung.

THE WEAVING OF A DREAM

I found this tale in a stunning American picture book entitled *The Weaving of a Dream* by Marilee Heyer. The retelling of the ancient Chinese folk tale *The Chuang Brocade* uses traditional features such as the journey, the number three and the rescuing power of the youngest son to full effect. It evokes potent pictures and visuals, and is a folk tale which has opened many intriguing doors in the classroom, particularly on the theme of dreams and desires.

Pronunciation notes
Leme – Lem-eh
Let uie – Let-oo-ee
Leje – Lej-eh

GLOSSARY OF DRAMA TECHNIQUES AND CONVENTIONS

A number of different drama techniques are employed in classroom storydrama to investigate a tale and 'dig down' into the story. The following résumé of the most commonly used techniques seeks to explain these conventions which provide structure to storydrama enquiries. Brief examples of the possible use of these techniques in relation to the retold tales in this book are provided. No priority is implied in this range of conventions; rather the teacher will select appropriate techniques to examine the issues, themes and spirit of a traditional tale as the drama unfolds.

Teacher in role: This is a central convention which enables the teacher to facilitate the drama and manage the learning opportunities from within it. The teacher adopts various roles at different points in the drama to challenge thinking, deepen commitment and create choices, ambiguity and tension. For example, in *The Children of Wax* (see pages 56–7), the teacher might adopt one or more of the following roles: mother, father, chief of the village, doctor, stranger or one of the children. Taking up such a role, through whole-group improvisation, the teacher can extend the children's thinking and their imaginative engagement in the storydrama experience.

Freeze-frames: These are still images or silent tableaux created by a group of children using their own bodies to synthesise a moment in the drama, or an idea or theme. Such tableaux can present a fragment in the past, present or future of the characters and can be titled with a succinct caption to highlight the meaning conveyed. This convention enables groups to convey far more than they would with words alone, and is useful to represent difficult situations such as fights or abstract concepts and ideas. For example, in *The Weaving of a Dream* (see pages 161–4), the children could make tableaux of the three sons' imaginary dreams or premonitions of what might have happened to their mother's beautiful brocade. Alternatively, at the close of a drama when the class tale has unfolded, groups could make freeze-frames which represent the issue or theme that *their* tale examined. The contrasting ideas and images which groups convey can be highlighted.

Whole-group role-play: Using this convention the class and their teacher spontaneously improvise their response to a situation. The drama unfolds as the group interact together and respond to the real and the symbolic tension and context. It is a useful and frequently used technique to develop personal and group engagement in a situation. For example, in *Ladder to the Sky* (see pages 11–12), the tale might be taken as a guide, and when the grandmother descends the vine and it crashes to the ground, the teacher/narrator could suggest the villagers rush to watch as their connection with the Great Manitou is severed. This situation could then be improvised, with a child or the teacher as the grandmother and others in the group adopting different roles and perspectives. The group have to manage this encounter as if it were actually happening and live with the consequences of their words and actions.

Small-group improvisation: In groups, the members of the class improvise some unknown aspect of the narrative – this may be spontaneous or a prepared improvisation. However, each improvisation is not watched by the rest of the class and only a very brief extract may be shared. The improvisation could be in the present, could create the future or re-create some incident in the past to seed ideas into the drama. For example, in *The Children of Wax* (see pages 56–7), the scene when the father builds his children a dark hut to live in could be improvised, and the attitudes and views of the children examined through small-group improvisations as each group take up the roles of father and children.

Interviews: Working in pairs or small groups, in role children interview a character from within a tale to elicit information. Their questions need to be well framed and brief snippets of these interrogations may be shared in the whole class context. In *The Final Victory* (see pages 95–6), for example, Tuk, the surviving hunter, could be interviewed formally by the tribal chief or the community law enforcer, or questioned more informally by his mother or trusted friends.

Communal meetings: These are held with the teacher, working in role, to allow the imaginary community, group or council to hear new information, discuss the situation, voice solutions, plan action and make corporate decisions. Meetings are a useful way to stimulate the consideration of alternatives and summarise the drama. For example, in *The Weaving of a Dream* (see pages 161–4), an imaginary council of the sun fairies could meet Leje to discuss his request for his mother's brocade.

Narration: The teacher can provide a narrative link between different moments examined with the drama through retelling aspects of action which have taken place and providing bridges forwards or backwards in the drama. Such narration can create atmosphere and tension and can give shape and form to the activity while honouring the children's ideas. For example, in examining *How the Crab got its Back* (see pages 128–9), the teacher may describe the land where the old woman lives: 'It was a strange ethereal place inhabited by all the mythical beings of the world – a land not here, not there, but in another place, another time – a land where magic was plotted, plans were hatched and the actions of humans on planet Earth were watched, commented upon and sometimes, oh yes, sometimes, interfered with. On this day the old woman had given Esmeralda's outer body the girl's inner beauty and when the old crone returned to her own land, well she...' Through such storytelling the teacher can prompt further dramatic investigation and arouse interest and involvement as well as make the drama more coherent.

Thinking out loud: Interior monologues can be voiced by individuals (or by the whole class in role) who represent particular characters thinking out loud about their hopes and fears at a particular moment in the drama. When the action is frozen and private thoughts are explored, a sensitive and more reflective response to the content is generated and insights into characters gained. For example, in *The End of Baba Yaga* (see pages 31–2), when Vasseila has been magically turned into a pin to escape Baba Yaga's clutches, her thoughts could be spoken aloud as night falls and she ponders on her predicament in the kitchen of the witch woman's abode.

Writing in/alongside role: This technique allows children to write during the drama (in role) or to write from a distance after the imagined experience of the drama (alongside role). In writing diaries, journals, logs and letters or producing messages, codes or postcards, children can reflect upon the experience, adopt appropriate language, write for 'real' audiences and establish alternative viewpoints. For example, in *The Children of Wax* (see pages 56–7), Ngwabi's diary entries as he dreams of freedom and listens to the flesh children's laughter could be written in role during a storydrama. Alternatively, at the close of the drama, newspaper accounts of the various events in the village which the class created could be produced.

Hot seating: In this convention one person or a small group is placed on the 'hot seat' as a character from the tale and is interviewed and questioned to establish further information about her background, behaviour and motivation. This can encourage a reflective awareness of human behaviour. For example, in *Ladder to the Sky* (see pages 11–12), the villagers could request an interview with a spirit messenger to establish whether the spirits of the Great Manitou have been favouring the young man. In this way the values and actions of the gods could be established, or the young man himself could be hot seated by members of the community.

Overheard conversations: These conversations may be undertaken in pairs or small groups and then snippets of them can be overheard in the drama to seed further ideas and offer explanations and perspectives. They are useful to consider the truth of rumours, the way in which 'tall' stories are created and to examine alternative perspectives about an event. For example, in *How the Sun Came into the World* (see pages 144–5), the animals could be overheard by the sky spirits discussing the strange phenomenon of light and the advantages of clear vision and warmth.

Decision line/thought line: This convention involves the class creating a two-sided line or pathway along which a character from the drama walks when confronted with a significant decision. As the character passes by, individuals voice the inner thoughts of the character and act as a collective conscience to advise and evaluate the situation. This both slows down the action to allow for deeper reflection and enables the complexity of choices to be examined. For example, in *Ladder to the Sky* (see pages 11–12), the grandmother's path around the village to the vine could be made and her conscience construed as she walks towards it. Should she break the laws of the community and ascend the vine after her grandson? Or accept his disappearance and remain alone on the earth? Her thoughts will be heard aloud as a member of the class, in role as the grandmother, walks slowly down the path. When she reaches the end of the path, the class can ask her for her decision. Which side of her conscience finally held sway?

Individual/collective drawing: Individuals or small groups draw an image of an object, place or group of people in the drama. This gives form to imagined components and encourages children to share their internal images and negotiate a common response. For example, individuals working on *The End of Baba Yaga* (see pages 31–2) as the character of Vasseila could 'find something intriguing' in the forest, and draw this in detail. Alternatively, as a group the portrait of Baba Yaga which hung over her mantelpiece in her house could be constructed, or a map of Vasseila's journey to the hut could be drawn.

Ritual/ceremony: This convention involves the group in creating a particular ceremony to mark a significant event. This will lean on cultural or historical knowledge and may involve performance of song, dance, music or poetry composed for the occasion or extracted from elsewhere. Rituals are useful to mark a moment and can involve everyone as a concluding element in a drama. For example, in *The Final Victory* (see pages 95–6), a ceremony to bury Nahnuk and celebrate his life could be devised and undertaken, with slow and ritual significance, reflecting both upon his strengths and apparent weaknesses.

BIBLIOGRAPHY

Alwyin, A. and Peters, J. (1989) *Children as Storytellers*, video cassette and booklet, Thames Polytechnic.

Alwyin, A. (1992) *Traditional Storytelling and Education*, University of Greenwich.

Baker, A. and Greene, E. (1996) *Storytelling: Art and Technique*, R.R. Bowker.

Barton, B. (1986) *Tell Me Another: Storytelling and Reading Aloud at Home, at School and in the Community*, Pembroke.

Bettelheim, B. (1991) *The Uses of Enchantment: The Meaning and Importance of Fairy Tales*, Penguin.

Bird, G. and Norris, J. (1986) *In on the Act: Work in English and Drama*, Oxford University Press.

Bolton, G. (1984) *Drama as Education: An Argument for Placing Drama at the Centre of the Curriculum*, Longman.

Booth, D. (1985) 'Imaginary Gardens with Real Toads', Reading and Drama in Education, *Theory into Practice* XXIV.

Booth, D. (1987) *Drama Words: The Role of Drama in Language Growth*, Toronto: Language Study Centre.

Booth, D. (1994) *Story Drama: Reading, Writing and Role-Playing Across the Curriculum*, Pembroke.

Brice Heath, S. (1983) *Ways with Words: Language, Life and Work in Communities and Classrooms*, Cambridge University Press.

Britton, J. (1982) in *Prospect and Retrospect: Selected Essays of James Britton*, ed. Prad, G., Heinemann.

Bruner, J. (1987) *Actual Minds, Possible Worlds*, Harvard University Press.

Bruner, J. (1988) 'Life as Narrative' in *Language Arts* 65.6.

Candappa, B. (1989) 'A Crackle of Excitement' in *By Word of Mouth: The Revival of Storytelling* by Medlicott, M., C4 Broadside Publications.

Cassirer, E. (1953) *The Philosophy of Symbolic Forms*, Yale University Press.

Centre for Learning in Primary Education (1993) *Stories in the Multicultural Classroom: Supporting Children's Learning of English as a Second Language*, Harcourt Brace Jovanovich Ltd.

Chambers, A. (1993) *Tell Me: Children Reading and Talk*, Thimble Press.

Chukovsky, K. (1963) *From Two to Five*, University of California Press.

Colum, P.(1948) in the introduction to *The Complete Grimms' Fairy Tales*, Routledge and Kegan Paul.

Colwell, E. (1991) *Storytelling*, Thimble Press.

Cook, E. (1969) *The Ordinary and The Fabulous: An Introduction to Myths, Legends and Fairy Tales*, Cambridge University Press.

DFE (1995), *Key Stages 1 and 2 of the National Curriculum*, HMSO.

DFE (1990) *Teaching and Learning of Drama*, HMSO.

Doonan, J. (1992) *Looking at Pictures in Picture Books*, Thimble Press.

Egan, K. (1988) *Teaching as Storytelling*, Routledge.

English and Media Centre (1984) *Making Stories*, NATE.

English and Media Centre (1984) *Changing Stories*, NATE.

Fairman, T. (1991) *Bury My Bones But Keep My Words*, Collins.

Foggin, J. (1992) *Real Writing*, Hodder & Stoughton.

Fox, C. (1990) 'The Genesis of Argument in Narrative Discourse' in *English in Education*, Vol. 24, No. 1, NATE.

Fox, C. (1993) *At the very Edge of the Forest: The Influence of Literature on Storytelling by Children*, Cassell.

Fry, D. (1985) *Children Talk about Books: Seeing Themselves as Readers*, Open University Press.

Glassie, H. (1986) *Irish Folk Tales*, Penguin.

Graham, J. (1990) *Pictures on the Page*, NATE.

Hardy, B. (1977) 'Towards a Poetics of Fiction: An Approach through Narrative' in *The Cool Web*, ed. Meek, M., Warlow, A., Barton, G., Bodley Head.

Heathcote, D. (1976) *Drama as a Learning Medium*, Wagner, B.J., Hutchinson.

Howe, A. and Johnson, J. (1992) *Common Bonds: Storytelling in the Classroom*, Hodder & Stoughton.

Iser, W. (1979) *The Act of Reading: A Theory of Aesthetic Response*, Hopkins Press.

Jones, P. (1988) *Lip Service: The Story of Talk in Schools*, Open University Press.

Lord, A. (1960) *The Singer of Tales*, Harvard University Press.

Mallan, K. (1991) *Children as Storytellers*, Primary English Teaching Association, Australia.

Martin, N., Williams, P., Wilding, J., Hemmings, S. and Medway, P. (1976) *Understanding Children Talking*, Penguin.

Medlicott, M. (ed.) (1989) *By Word of Mouth: The Revival of Storytelling*, C4 Broadside Publications.

Meek, M. (1988) *How Texts Teach What Children Learn*, Thimble Press.

Meek, M. (1990) *On Being Literate*, Bodley Head.

Moffett, J. (1968) *Teaching the Universe of Discourse*, Houghton Mifflin.

Neelands, J. (1984) *Making Sense of Drama*, Heinemann.

Neelands, J. (1992) *Learning through Imagined Experience*, Hodder & Stoughton.

Ong, W. (1990) *Orality and Literacy: The Technologizing of the Word*, Routledge.

Paley, V.G. (1981) *Wally's Stories*, Harvard University Press.

Paley, V.G. (1990) *The Boy who wanted to be a Helicopter*, Harvard University Press.

Parkinson, R. (1996) *Storylines*, Society for Storytelling, Vol. 3, No. 1.

Pellowski, A. (1990) *The World of Storytelling: A Practical Guide to the Origins, Development and Application of Storytelling*, H.W. Wilson Co.

Propp, V. (1968) *The Morphology of the Folktale*, University of Texas.

Reece, J. (1996) *The Teller, the Tales and Countless Interpretations*, Unpublished MA thesis, Canterbury Christ Church College.

Rimmon-Kenan, S. (1983) *Narrative Fiction: Contemporary Poetics*, Methuen.

Rosen, B. (1988) *And None of it was Nonsense: The Power of Story in School*, Mary Glasgow.

Rosen, B. (1993) *Shapers and Polishers: Teachers as Storytellers*, Mary Glasgow.

Rosen, H. (1984) *Stories and Meanings*, NATE.

Rosen, H. (1988) 'Postscript' in *And None of it was Nonsense*, Mary Glasgow.

Rosen, H. (1988) 'Stories of Stories' in *The Word for Teaching is Learning*, Martin, N. and Lightfoot, G., Heinemann.

Rosen, H. (1993) *Troublesome Boy*, English and Media Centre.

Rule, H. and Goodman, S. (1979) *Gulpilil's Stories of the Dreamtime*, William Collins, Sydney.

Rushdie, S. (1991) *Haroun and the Sea of Stories*, Granta Books.

Sawyer, R. (1962) *The Way of the Storyteller*, Bodley Head.

SCAA (1995) *One Week in March: A Survey of the Literature Pupils Read:* Paper No. 4, SCAA.

SCAA (1995) *Planning the Curriculum at Key Stages 1 and 2*, SCAA

Simms, L. (1982) 'Storytelling, Children and Imagination', *The Yarnspinner*, Vol. 6, No. 2, Heinemann.

Smith, F. (1992) *To Think in Language Learning and Education*, Routledge.

Society for Storytelling (1996) *Storytelling in Education*, The Arts Council.

Steele, M. (ed.) (1988) *Traditional Tales*, Thimble Press.

Stenhouse, L. (1975) *An Introduction to Curriculum Research and Development*, Heinemann.

Taylor, M. (1994) 'What Children's Books Tell Us About Teaching Language' in *The Prose and The Passion* by Styles, M., Bearne, E. and Watson, V., Cassell.

Vygotsky, L. (1978) *Mind in Society*, Harvard University Press.

Wade, B. (1984) *Story at Home and School*, Birmingham Education Review.

Weir, L. (ed.) (1988) *Telling the Tale: A Storytelling Guide*, Pamphlet No. 29, The Library Association Youth Libraries Group.

Wells, G. (1987) *The Meaning Makers: Children Learning Language and Using Language to Learn*, Hodder & Stoughton.

Wells, G. and Nicholls, J. (1985) *Language and Learning: An International Perspective*, Falmer.

Wilkinson, A., Davies, A. and Berrill, D. (1990), *Spoken English Illuminated*, Open University Press.

Zipes, F. (1996) *Creative Storytelling: Building Community, Changing Lives*, Routledge.

Zipes, J. (1995) *Fairy Tales and The Art of Subversion*, Routledge.

INDEX

animals 23, 25, 85, 134–5, 139
anthologies 48, 142, 147
    class 135; folk tales 131; with
    music 157; written/taped 76, 138
asides 159
assessment 130, 133, 138
audience(s)
    awareness 81; beginnings and
    endings 150; commitment 147;
    different 37, 71, 135; interaction
    20, 30, 36, 49–50, 71, 155–7;
    involvement 158–60; multiple 138;
participation 81, 152, 154;
    power and influence 75; in
projects 138; range of 140; sense
    of 43–4; for storytelling 50, 61;
    for writing 54, 123

ballads 24
beginnings and endings 72–4, 102–4
    and audience 81; changing 84;
    language of 29; recording 149,
    150–1; traditional 83

characters 64, 79
    emotions graphs 60, 87–8, 90;
    fictional 117, 118–20; investigating
85–90; ladders 87; legendary
local 133; maps 86; puppet 125;
    and retelling 72, 75; typical 83
communal meetings 47, 105, 109, 159
communication 37, 43, 132
conferences 41, 43, 127
    storytelling 65, 78–9, 80–1, 91, 137
conversations, overheard 109
curriculum, storytelling in 130–43

drama 42, 53–4, 58, 85, 124–7
    techniques 70, 86, 99, 100–1,
    104, 108 *see also* storydrama
drawing, individual/collective 19,
    63–70, 107, 118, 122

English Centre 84
epics 24, 29
expression, facial 78, 80–1, 125,
    149, 155–6, 159
extension activities 99, 107–8, 113–16,
    134–7, 139

fables 22, 24, 132
fairy tales *see* folk and fairy tales
family stories 22, 35, 61, 133, 135, 146
fantasy 27, 36, 55, 83
flashbacks/flash forwards 102
folk and fairy tales 9, 19, 22–3, 30, 147
    animal 134–5, 139; characters 87,
    90; in continuing work 130;
    conventions 45–6; in events and
    festivals 141; forgotten 85;
    invented 24; in national
    curriculum 48; nature of 83–4;
    in projects 132–6; and psychology
    25–6; and puppetry 125–7;
    reading 63; stereotyping in 26–7;
    in storydrama 54, 98, 102;
    structures 27–8
folklore 27, 84, 140
    children's 59; family 8–9, 61, 146;
    fictional 63–4; in role-play areas
    118, 119–20; in storydrama 10, 98,
    99, 104; in storytelling 30, 62, 142
freeze–frames 100, 102, 104, 105,
    110, 112–13

games 63, 73
gesture 78, 79, 80–1, 149, 153,
    155–6, 160

heroes and heroines 87, 137, 139
    traditional 17, 22, 24, 83
hot seating 70, 86, 100–1, 111–12

improvisation 54, 111–12, 116
    small-group 100, 110, 117, 121–2,
    124–5, 127; in storydrama 100,
    101, 102–4
interior monologues 70, 86, 110–11
interviews 105

journeys 25, 28, 63, 67, 69, 105, 158

keyword summaries 66, 149

language 8, 35, 50, 82
    competence 60; figurative 46, 91;
    formal 51; learning 9–10; and role-
play areas 122–3; second 42,
156–7; spoken 16, 42–3, 123;